The Wicked   John Goode

Horace Winthrop Scandlin

HEATHEN EDITIONS
THEIR BOOKS. OUR WAY.

Published in the good ole United States of America
by Heathen Editions, an imprint of
Heathen Creative
P.O. Box 588
Point Pleasant, WV 25550-0588

Heathen Editions are available at quantity discounts.
For information and more tomfoolery, check us out online:

heatheneditions.com

@heatheneditions
#heathenedition

First serialized in *The Christian Herald* November 1916 – January 1917
First published in book form March 1917
Heathen Edition published May 7, 2023

Book and cover design by Sheridan Cleland
Set in 11pt Plantin Std
Chapters in Tox Typewriter

ISBN: 978-1-948316-44-6

FIRST HEATHEN EDITION

"Every minister in the United States should have a copy of this book." —*The Christian Herald*

"It is about the most convincing story in the brand-from-the-burning line that has come along." —*St. Louis Post-Dispatch*

"A narrative, true in every particular, of almost incredible depravity, degradation, and squalor; and of a yet more unbelievable rescue and reformation. The age of miracles is *not* past. A product of the foul underworld becomes a child of the Light." —*Methodist Review*

"These are the two chief points in this remarkable story of John Goode's youth and early manhood—the marvel of his fall and rise, and the lesson that his experience holds in its sad commentary upon the institutions and the efforts at 'reform' which touched John Goode's life. Personally and socially, this is a suggestive and challenging book." —*The New York Times Book Review*

"Here is an astonishing narrative. A plain, unvarnished tale with a glory that demonstrates anew the redemptive and transforming power of Christ. John Goode was everything that was evil—a drunkard, a jail-bird, a thief. Today he is one of the leaders of the famous Bowery Mission. This story of his redemption blazes with the light of the Cross—a final and perfect answer to every doubting Thomas who cries for 'proof.'" —*The Book News Monthly*

"Here we have a 'vital document' out of the real life of the Bowery Mission in New York. The portrait shows us the face of a genuine man; the tale matches the rugged countenance. The story is told with fine reserve; there is no maudlin sentiment about it but rather the deep sincerities of a true and self-revealing soul. This is an experience that reveals the power of genuine Christianity. We commend this book to everyone who craves a fresh breath of sincerity and conviction and who is ready to have his heart kindled by another chapter of the acts of Christ." —*The Biblical World*

When I was a child, I spake as a child,
I understood as a child, I thought as a
child: but when I became a man, I put
away childish things.

For now we see through a glass,
darkly; but then face to face: now
I know in part; but then shall I know
even as also I am known.

1 Corinthians 13:11-12

Contents

Heathenry:
Thoughts on the Text

Here, we present another compelling nonfiction addition to our Convictions Series following *My Life in Prison* by Donald Lowrie, *Within Prison Walls* by Thomas Mott Osborne, and *The Story of Canada Blackie*.

What's more, John Goode name-drops all three and was directly linked to two: Osborne contributed the introduction for this book and, while he doesn't state it in this story, Goode and Canada Blackie were imprisoned at Sing Sing at the same time.

But what makes John Goode's story intriguing, and by degrees vastly different from those of other reformed criminals from the "new penology" era, is that John Goode, stubborn knucklehead though he was, didn't just ultimately "make good," he reformed by devoting his life to God.

Although he needed real convincing because his wasn't a spiritual "flip of the switch" transformation; once he was on the path to redemption, Goode stumbled and fell many times, but — and this is the crucial part — every time he got back up he was even more convinced than before that he was on the *right* path.

1 Corinthians 13, Goode's favorite Bible chapter, tells

us that Love is patient — "Charity suffereth long" says the King James Version — and it was that patience exhibited by the leaders of the Bowery Mission, and that long suffering physically embodied in his frail wife that eventually shored up his resolve, cemented his conviction, and truly made him a brand plucked out of the fire.

It was also at the Bowery Mission that Horace Winthrop Scandlin first met John Goode, and when Scandlin heard Goode's story he knew it had to be told, so *The Wicked John Goode* was serialized in twelve parts in *The Christian Herald*, where Scandlin was then an associate editor, from November 1916 to January 1917 as follows:

- November 1: Chapters 1–2
- November 8: Chapters 3–6
- November 15: Chapters 6–9
- November 22: Chapters 9–12
- November 29: Chapters 12–13
- December 6: Chapters 13–15
- December 13: Chapters 16–17
- December 20: Chapters 17–18
- December 27: Chapters 19–20
- January 3: Chapter 21
- January 10: Chapter 22
- January 17: Chapter 23 and Epilogue

So strong was the positive reaction to John Goode's story that it saw quick publication in book form in March 1917.

Now, as for the text, we have updated some hyphened words to their modern equivalents: to-day is now today, good-bye has become goodbye, and so on. And since Goode and Scandlin were both American, we have swapped many British words for their American counterparts: realise is now realize, labour is now labor, and so on.

The bulk of our work, however, lies in the 80 footnotes that we've appended throughout the text to provide context, clarity, and commentary where needed.

In addition to the Introduction by Thomas Mott Osborne and the Epilogue by Rev. John G. Hallimond, which were included in the original book, *The Christian Herald* featured some ancillary articles during the story's serialization which we found relevant enough to include here as well.

The first is "Love" by Arthur H. Howland, which digs into the Bible chapter that forever altered John Goode's life, 1 Corinthians 13, and dissects its use of the word "charity" in the King James Version.

The second is "The Mission of John Goode," an editorial answer to a question about the serial posed by a reader of *The Christian Herald* concerning "the wisdom and spiritual profit of publishing the characters of bad men."

We believe both articles are spot-on in their analyses.

We have also included, as appendices, three articles that Scandlin wrote for another religious magazine, *World Outlook*,[1] which details his thoughts on the "prison problem" as it existed at the time and relays some stories he heard while mingling with ex-cons on the streets of New York City.

Finally, on the last page, we've included a few letters from *Christian Herald* readers who reacted to the serial upon its conclusion in 1917.

Perhaps you will share their opinions?

P.S. If you're not familiar with us or our books, then a quick explanation may be in order, especially given the subject matter of this book, as the "heathen" of Heathen Editions has nothing to do with religion (or lack of it) and everything to do with cats, because in the parts of Appalachia from which we hail "heathen" is often used as a term of endearment, and we love our cats — nay *heathens!* — so much that it just made sense to name this publishing venture after them.

---

[1] *World Outlook*, the official mission magazine of The United Methodist Church, began publication in 1911, then changed its name to *New World Outlook* in February 1968, before ceasing publication in October 2018.

Introduction

Recalling my early reading of Aesop's Fables, I always enjoyed the moral at the end of each story; for then I felt quite sure I had understood; and I liked to be quite certain of that.

In that most delightful of nursery classics, *Alice in Wonderland*,[1] one of the characters gravely remarks: "Everthing's got a moral if only you can find it."[2] I confess to an increasing desire, as the years advance, to find the moral of things.

In the story of John Goode one can find several good morals, but the one that appeals most to me might be worded thus: Take care of the boy and the man will take care of himself.

Do what we will, there will always be need of correctional institutions to care for those who, for some reason or other, cannot or will not play the game of life according to the rules laid down by the community — "Society Misfits." Whether it is their fault, or the fault of their ancestors, or of the environment, matters little to the public which suffers from their

---

[1] *Alice's Adventures in Wonderland* is an 1865 English novel by English author, poet, and mathematician Lewis Carroll (1832–1898).
[2] Spoken by the Duchess in Chapter 9: The Mock Turtle's Story.

destructive activity. When the law lays its hands upon these mischief-makers it sends them to some institution; and when they make trouble there we call them "incorrigibles," thus assuming that it must be the fault of the inmates rather than of the institution.

*

John Goode, at the age of ten, was an "incorrigible"; so he tells us. But was he? Suppose he had found, in one of the institutions to which he was sent, an intelligent system which would have stimulated his sense of honor and his capacity to bear responsibility, as well as a superintendent who was a sympathetic teacher; can one doubt that the inherent strength and goodness of the man, which at last has seized upon him and now dominates him, would have emerged then? Are we to suppose that the sacred fire cannot be kindled in these men until the soul has been smirched? Perhaps if I had not seen young boys as incorrigible as John Goode ever was at the age of ten, turned by humane and sensible treatment into good and useful citizens, I should think otherwise; but having beheld with my own eyes the gradual but complete reformation of many such youthful delinquents, long before I saw the same thing among the adult prisoners of Auburn and Sing Sing, I know that there was no reason for John Goode's early failure to reform, except the stupid maladministration of the institutions which received him bad and made him worse. It is only another case where "Man's inhumanity to man makes countless thousands mourn."

*

In the course of time John Goode reformed. But the reform of an individual criminal here and there is no new thing. It may happen, and has happened, in any one of several ways — among them the way it happened to John Goode. But one of the important lessons to us is that it did not happen through the agency of any one of the institutions in which he was placed. Every one of them made a failure of him. As the event showed, he was good material all the while; yet so far as society's official agencies of reform were concerned he was the worst for all of them. And such conditions should be a matter of shame to us. Think of the many years of life wasted and worse than wasted, in which the man's strength might have been used for the benefit of society, instead of toward its destruction! Also think of the thousands whom the light never strikes as it struck John Goode.

The chief moral, therefore, which I find in this story deals with the obligation that is upon us to reform the reformatory institutions to which our little John Goodes are sent and which are now little else than feeders to our state prisons. Every state has juvenile refuges and children's protectories and industrial schools and reformatories. I have heard of very few which allow the children enough initiative to enable them to prepare themselves thoroughly and efficiently for life. We swing from brutality to benevolent paternalism; and while the latter is pleasanter, it is almost as harmful.

In the meantime, let us be grateful that we have occasional John Goodes, strong enough to seek and find God in spite of the barriers we ignorantly and stupidly place in their way.

THOMAS MOTT OSBORNE [3]

---

[3] Thomas Mott Osborne (1859–1926) was an American prison administrator, prison reformer, industrialist, and New York State political reformer. In 1912, he was inspired to read *My Life in Prison* by Donald Lowrie, a former inmate of San Quentin State Prison in California, which he pinpointed as the genesis of his prison reform crusade. The following year he was appointed chairman of a new State Commission on Prison Reform, then spent six days of imprisonment as "Tom Brown" in Auburn Prison. He recorded his experiences in his 1914 book *Within Prison Walls* — now available as a Heathen Edition! — whose publication made him the most prominent prison reform crusader of his day. The following year he was appointed warden of Sing Sing.

Love

Some newspaper readers remember even yet an incident of a Staten Island courtroom which occurred about fifteen years ago. A man whose name was Goode was being sentenced to state prison. In passing sentence the judge said: "Your name is Goode, but it ought to be Bad," and then proceeded to give the prisoner a tongue-lashing such as is rarely heard in a courtroom. For this man was not only bad, thus belying the beautiful name with which he had been born, but his badness was of a peculiarly despicable character. It has often been said that there is honor even among thieves, but even among the crooks of New York this man was considered too crooked to be tolerated. He was yellow, mean, thoroughly and desperately bad.

But now this same man is one of the most faithful and efficient Christian workers in New York City. He has entered into the inheritance of his beautiful name. Some of his companions think that he is not only good, but best; and one friend particularly speaks of him as the best Christian he knows.

What changed John Goode from the worst of the bad to the best of the good? If the answer had to be limited to one item, one single object, it would the Thirteenth Chapter of First Corinthians. For six months the Bible class of the Bowery Mission Brotherhood studied that wonderful chapter under the leadership of Dr. Hallimond,[1] and John Goode, who with all his contact with the world had never realized that there was such a thing as love, was changed from a sinner to a saint.

Professor Drummond was not guilty of exaggeration in calling love The Greatest Thing in the World. It is the basis, the atmosphere, the method, the power of all goodness.

The Thirteenth Chapter of First Corinthians brought to the world what was really a new word. Of course the word love was in the ancient languages, but it never meant to the ancient pagan or even to the Jew what it means to the Christian. Love, as the ancient poets used it, meant often a very cruel sort of selfishness, a selfishness that would sacrifice to its desire the virtue, the welfare, the happiness of another. They used the word love in much the same childish sense that children use it when they speak of loving something that they like to eat. The pagan idea of love was the desire to possess and enjoy, which became often the desire to destroy and devour. But the love of parent for child, of child for parent, of friend for friend, of husband for wife, was even in those days a real and beautiful thing. The Jews added to that idea of human love the thought of love and loyalty to God. But Christian love means a love for others that grows out of our love for Christ; or perhaps we should say a love for Christ that expresses itself in ardent, happy, self-sacrificing love for others. And there is always in the highest idea of Christian love the thought of the cross of Christ. People who really believe that Jesus died for them have necessarily a deeper, more vital, more intense love for him than those could have who do not. That is in all their thought and feeling about

[1] John Greener Hallimond D.D. (1852–1924) was an English-born pastor and author who in 1900 became superintendent of the Bowery Mission, the oldest Christian rescue mission in New York City, where he remained until his death on November 21, 1924.

him: "He died for me." And because he died for them he is dear to them.

This is how that old word "charity" crept into this chapter in the King James version, instead of love. High school Latin pupils will recognize this word charity "caritas." *Caritas* really means the feeling one has when another is *dear* to him (*carus*). So Christian love is a feeling, or emotion, that one has when Christ is dear to him; and dear to him because he manifested his own love by suffering and death. Then because of the dearness of Christ, because the Christian really loves him and wishes to please him, and because Christ died for all, the Christian feels that people are dear, are precious; he loves all, and tries to help all.

Paul sums this up in a beautiful passage in Second Corinthians, chapter 5:14-15: "For the love of Christ constraineth us; because we thus judge, that if one died for all, then were all dead: and that he died for all, that they which live should not henceforth live unto themselves, but unto him which died for them, and rose again."

It is this kind of love, Christian love, love that springs up in the heart of those whom Jesus has redeemed, that is going to change and save this bad world just as it saved that man John Goode and made him even better than his name.

ARTHUR H. HOWLAND[2]

---

[2] Arthur Hoag Howland (1873–1952) was a Method minister, journalist, and editor who worked briefly as the associate editor of the *Christian Herald*.

The Mission of John Goode

A reader in New Hampshire questions the wisdom and spiritual profit of publishing the characters of bad men. "I have always been instructed," he says, "that the contemplation of vice and crime was dangerous. Have I been taught wrong? Even if the outcome of the story of wicked John Goode is glorious, it does not, according to my mind, render it safe reading for the young, in earlier life especially. I have taken the *Christian Herald* for many years, and sincerely love and value it."

As there are no doubt others who may have asked themselves the same question, we take this opportunity of saying that we are not at all surprised at criticism of the autobiography. John Goode's story is a confession of sin, a confession so truthful and unsparing that it cannot fail to impress all who read it. It is not food for babes, but strong meat for men, who need just such a vivid, forceful presentation to warn them. John Goode has bared his own soul, that his experience may arrest others who have entered on the path that leads to destruction. He knows that road and the perils it holds for those who travel there. And he knows the only way out of danger, and is now spending his life in saving others.

The highest of all examples, the Bible itself, both the Old Testament and the New, pictures sin in its true colors. It may be shocking to some sensitive minds, but there it is. The purpose is clearly to make sin's vileness and hideousness apparent to all, to show how it defaces and even effaces all that is noble in humanity; to demonstrate how absolute is the domination of evil over one who has forgotten God and given himself wholly over to the lusts of the flesh. We confess that we ourselves do not like the picture; no one can like it. It is drastic, repelling, shocking. But here comes the miracle. We turn in loathing from such men and, when we look back at them again, find to our astonishment that divine grace has touched even their vile hearts, and that wonderful change has begun in their lives. Could there be in the life of today a greater or more convincing demonstration to the world of the Gospel truth that "He saves to the uttermost,"[1] than in such a case as that of John Goode?

We must remember that Christianity is not a life of shelter, seclusion, and privileged association, and that the church is something more than a collection of saints, who must not be shocked by violent contact with human depravity. It is the duty of every Christian to remember the injunction to go out into the highways and byways, to seek the outcast, the criminal, the imprisoned, the hopeless; to be "all things to all men,"[2] if by any means he may save some. And we believe the challenge of John Goode's life and experience is one that should arouse self-satisfied Christians to a sense of duty to those who are down in the depths.

[1] Hebrews 7:25
[2] 1 Corinthians 9:19-23

The Wicked John Goode

1.
My Start

It was cold and sharp with wind and the snow crunched crisply underfoot as host and guest entered the grounds of a modest and comfortable country home. The log fire in the cozy living room burned cheerfully and cast a soft, mellow light halfway into the room as the two men dropped into huge leather chairs invitingly placed before it. They awaited the call to dinner. Weary and footsore they were after a five mile jaunt from the club where they had spent the morning.

With keen appetites the two men partook of a roast and its fixings in silence.

Each seemed absorbed with his own reflections. Reaction after the walk perhaps, or was it the season? It was the last day of the year. Was it the year they were about to leave behind, the years they had left behind, or the year they were about to enter of which these two men were thinking? At any rate, their silence remained unbroken. They seemed to understand — these two men — the silence seemed as satisfying as the meal.

Coffee and cheese were served at a small table in front of the fireplace amid the still unbroken silence. And as if to hold unbroken their reverie they settled deep down in their chairs.

The guest was massive — a giant of New England origin developed into rugged manhood by a strenuous early life in the far and middle West. Close cropped hair — gray — and deep facial lines indicated his age as sixty-five, but the huge unbent frame and the steel like muscles of the big limbs seemed not more than forty. The high and heavy forehead and the overhanging brow bespoke intellect. The keen, steel blue eyes spelled determination. Yet those eyes had a soft, kindly look, one that invited confidence. It was a look not at all like what one would associate with the rest of the portrait. A square protruding chin completed the picture of a man who could and would indulge and who had indulged his every desire.

The guest drew from his pocket a package of papers and extracted a typewritten letter which he read and re-read many times.

"That's an invitation to speak at a Men's Club," he said quietly as though continuing aloud a mental conversation.

"I've done a pile of thinking ever since it came. Last night Dr. Hallimond asked me to be sure and accept it. Of course I'll do anything he asks.

"As I look back sometimes — like today, for instance — it seems as though I must be dreaming or as though Aladdin had crossed my path. Just think of all the friends I've got. Just think what you've all meant to me and who you all are — businessmen, doctors, lawyers, ministers, editors, scores of you, and look at me!

"I'm a porter,[1] ten hours a day, eleven dollars a week, 52 years old and — and — " The sentence remained unfinished.

I hesitated about replying, for I knew well the man and his manners. If I spoke the wrong reply I would divert the trend of his thoughts. So I kept silent, knowing instinctively I was to hear again as remarkable a story as was ever told —

---

[1] A person employed to carry luggage, parcels, etc., especially in a railway station, airport, or hotel.

a story of absolute truth and one that would do both teller and hearer much good.

And then John Goode began and told me for the second time this tale.

★

"I was two years old when my parents took me from Massachusetts to a silver camp, the town of Caribou in the northern part of the state of Colorado.[2] She — my mother — was a good woman. My father was a fighting, whiskey-drinking Irishman, as irritable when sober as he was cruel and vicious when drunk. I very rarely saw him when he was sober. He was a bad actor and had left Canada some years earlier just in time to escape the noose in a good stout rope. The town was sixty miles from the nearest railroad and the only Bible it contained was my mother's. My mother also had the distinction of being the only woman in that camp in the early days.

"Before long other children were born to my parents and as my mother's duties were many besides caring for her children I need not tell you that my early training was a totally minus quantity. My parents kept a boarding house for miners and you can easily imagine the environment I found myself in and how much attention my mother could give to us. There simply was no discipline. I grew up — that's all.

"In those days a mining camp was no fit place for children. All that these camps knew was rough work, rough people, rough times. Everything was hard.

"I'll never forget how in two winters two of my younger brothers and one sister died. The men, my father, and a friend built tiny coffins out of pine soap boxes which I fetched from the store. In these crude, rough, unlined affairs they placed the little bodies and then nailed on the lids. In each instance

---

[2] Caribou, situated northwest of Denver and west of Boulder, is a ghost town today, but the population was estimated at 3,000 during its peak in 1875.

ch. ends p. 6

the death occurred in winter and the frost was deep in the ground. Before the graves could be opened huge fires were built on the selected spots. We waited, my mother, father, and me with a few friends till the ground thawed out. No stone or wood marked these graves. No enclosure protected the little bodies. Soon even the little mounds had disappeared, and not long after that the incidents themselves were forgotten, for it was work, work, work of the hardest sort, with no time or place for sentiment or sorrow.

"Nor was there time or place for discipline. When we were well we kept out of the way. When we were sick we were a trouble, but in the crude manner of the day and place we were cared for and restored to health or we died.

"Had there been time for discipline it would have had no effect on me. My father blocked all efforts at anything but work. The only times he noticed me was when I crossed him in some childish way and then he beat me unmercifully. I soon learned that it was safest to keep out of his way, and thus it was that I also learned to know what 'father' meant. My hatred of him grew apace while my love for my mother — if I knew then what love meant — deepened. I remember her as a meek, quiet, sorrowful woman — a woman of few words. She always shielded me as best she could from my father and covered up my misdeeds. The beatings he gave me hurt her as much as they hurt me. I can vividly remember her pleading with him to be merciful as he brought a stick down on my bare back, blow after blow. Sometimes after she had lied to save me, a neighbor would tell him and then I would pay dearly for my wrong and for my mother's intended kindness.

"By the time I was seven I had learned well the need of keeping out of my father's sight and I had learned still better how to take care of myself. I had done my first stealing before I was five years old. I had helped myself to money from the cash drawer of the only store in camp. Why shouldn't I? I didn't know it was wrong! All I knew was that I couldn't get candy at home. There most of the money went for whis-key. No one saw me steal the first time or the second time, so no one scolded me. No one beat me for stealing, so it couldn't be wrong, my child mind reasoned.

"At ten I was incorrigible! I had felt my own power. I had experienced every sensation, good and bad, the town was able to supply. Caribou had become too small and my father too cruel. I had never been to school, for there was no school to go to! And so I reached the age of eleven — a liar and a thief!

"With that year came the most brutal beating a boy ever received. It developed into a fight — father and son. I was well put up and well versed with my hands and he was beastly drunk and mad. With that beating came an instant deter-mination to run away. Never for an instant would I regret leaving home — my brothers and sisters — my father and mother. What were they to me? Had I not shifted for myself all my life?[3] I could continue to do so.

"I walked the sixty miles to the railroad, to the then little wooden city of saloons, gambling houses, and dens of ill repute called Denver. It was fed then by but one railroad — the old Kansas Pacific, now the Union Pacific.

"I remember the thrills as they chased themselves up and down my spine when from a mountain top, afar off, I caught my first glimpse of the city.

"It was a walk I'll never forget. Bears and Indians and wolves were plentiful, and it was a trip that would test the nerves of the bravest boy. The long, long daylight hours and the dreadful, fearful thought of those surely coming nights with inky, inky blackness. . . . But little did I realize that the blackness of those black nights on that runaway journey were as broad daylight compared to the blackness of the life I was slowly but surely walking into.

"I was on the road four days and three nights. I slept on the ground two nights and in a deserted mining shack the other.

---

[3] To "shift for oneself" is to manage or make do as best as one can without help.

ch. ends next p.

I can distinctly remember the howling of the wolves and how lonely and frightened I was. But not once was I tempted to return to my father. He had taught me too well his lessons. All during the trip I had been fearful lest he should seek me, knowing, of course, that Denver was the only place to which I could head.

"I wonder if he made any effort to find me? I wonder what my mother thought and how she felt? Never once since I passed through the camp on my way to the railroad have I seen my father nor even heard of him. He must have long since passed over the Great Divide, for his manner of living fifty years ago could only have meant an early end. I have seen my mother only twice since and she too, no doubt, has passed to her reward. All that I ever knew of her life was hard, cruelly hard. No woman could stand it long.

2.
An Eleven-Year-Old Runaway!

"On leaving the mountains and dropping onto the plain in which is Denver I proceeded slowly, walking twice around it before entering or speaking to anyone. After I had sized up the place, I singled out what looked to be a boarding house and applied for a job. My surmise proved to be correct and I was set to work at once washing dishes. I didn't like the place nor the work, which was the first I'd ever done, and so after three days I beat it. As nothing had been said about wages, none were due me.

"I went to the railroad yard and picked up an acquaintance with an engineer who took my cock and bull story in whole. He was a good man and readily consented to my riding in the caboose of his freight leaving that day for Kansas City. My reception on the train of fifty odd freight cars and one caboose was cordial. My age of course was responsible for that.

"'Where yer going, son?'

"'Where yer been?'

"'Yer hungry?'

"The ice was broken. They took me in and shared their grub and bunks with me. Here I again experienced what I now know to be kindness. It made me feel queer. Here were all these rough looking, dirty men — and no one hit me — no one was drunk. They told me stories of railroading as it was done in those days, of holdups, of wrecks, and my blood fairly raced through my system, propelled by the beats of a little eleven-year-old runaway heart.

"I'm not telling you this for sympathy, God knows I'm not! I'm telling it to you so that the next time you are told of a man who is a criminal and who will never be anything else, remember my story and of the inherent good there was in me and is in every other human being, of how that little bit of goodness was kindled into flame — of how that little flame was nursed until it could keep aglow alone. Remember my start in life, perhaps the other fellow's start was like mine. I was as yellow a cur[1] as ever lived — a man couldn't be more yellow — and yet I had what every mortal has — an inherent grain of goodness that's God-given and which no man has the right to deny.

"In four days the train pulled onto a siding[2] in the freight yards at Kansas City. It had reached the end of its journey.

"Where was I going?

"I did not know.

"I had heard my mother say she had a sister in Massachusetts. I made up my mind then that I would go to her. At that time I had no idea I was different from any normal boy. There had been no means of my knowing that the life I was leading would take me to state's prison or the gallows, unless it was checked. I didn't know there was such a thing as a prison and gallows. But I learned about them soon enough. Then, however, I was just a healthy boy running away to escape a father's uncontrollable temper and desire for whiskey. I was on a train of freight cars and the men knew why I was there. They treated me kindly. But three days of kind treatment on a freight train won't alter a boy's character. Perhaps if I

---

[1] A cowardly and despicable person.

[2] A short section of railroad track connected at one or both ends to a main track.

had met men on leaving that freight gang, who treated me as they did, this sort of a story would never have been told. But I didn't meet the same sort of men.

"I met men and boys who like myself couldn't or wouldn't or didn't recognize the difference between right and wrong. I met men whose business it was to teach young boys to steal and pick pockets just as carefully as your boy is being taught how to become a manly man and, just like your boy, I learned my lessons well. I met other men who took these boys, when they had become expert, onto the road to steal and plunder and for other unspeakable purposes.

"As I say I learned my lessons well. I was an apt pupil — had begun early. My age was with me, for who would suspect an eleven year old boy of being a thief?

"I didn't stay long in Kansas City. I don't know why, except that way back somewhere in my head was that wish to go to my mother's sister. I beat my way to St. Louis on the Missouri Pacific. Sometimes I rode in coaches, more often underneath. Sometimes I begged my food, sometimes I stole to procure it, but the point is I always got it. Back door and front door alike yielded all the food I asked. Always my age and story brought the lady of the house across. And each time I told the story I added more sob stuff. Open windows and cellar doors got me all else I needed.

"And then the inevitable happened. Why it hadn't happened sooner I can't understand.

3.
My First Arrest — Age Eleven

"I made St. Louis late at night and forced a window in a stable. Crawling into a warm corner of the hay I was soon fast asleep. Toward morning the owner of the building and a cop appeared. I was picked up for entry and further accused of threatening to set fire to the premises!

"The Judge before whom I was arraigned tried as well as he knew how to show me the folly of my ways. I wonder if he had boys of his own. I hope not. I wonder how many other boys had previously been brought before him. I wonder how many followed me into his kindly considerate hands. What a story the history of all those lives would probably make could they now be written.

"He listened carefully to the charges they preferred against me — that one paid officer of the law and that big man, the owner of the stable — the charges they preferred against me, an unknown child.

"Instantly he made up his mind — he knew at once just the best way to handle my case — how best to put me in the frame of mind not to go into another man's stable to sleep. Why shouldn't this man — this judge — know what to do with me? Hadn't he been practicing on other boys for years?

"And so this judge — this man who had taken an oath to administer justice impartially to all who came before him, told me in open court before many people that I was a worthless, vicious boy — that there wasn't room for me in his city, and he wound up his tirade by giving me the privilege of leaving the city for good within twenty-four hours or of being sent away for a year. I chose the former.

"Picture that crime against me!

"Imagine such a man as that holding down such a job!

"He practically said to me that morning in court 'You're helpless and worthless. You'll never be any good. You belong in prison, but get out of here. We don't want to clog our jails with the likes of you. Get out of St. Louis. Go somewhere else and break the law there — not here.'

"I crossed the river to East St. Louis on a boat. I don't think the bridge had been built then. A freight on the Ohio and Mississippi, now the B&O,[1] was pulling out and I made it.

"I got as far as Sandoval, Illinois,[2] before the crew found me and put me off. Night was falling and the men working about the fires let me lie down in the warm sand, where I was soon fast asleep. They evidently suspected I was a waif,[3] for they saved scraps of bread and meat from their dinner pails, which I ate with great relish in the morning. Between the time the night shift quit and the day gang went on I was on my way afoot down the railroad tracks. At Odin, about five miles distant, a man stopped me on the main street and asked me who I was and where I was going. He was Levi Meredith, the county surveyor.[4] My size or, rather, lack of it and my dilapidated appearance interested him. I assumed

---

[1] The Baltimore and Ohio Railroad was the first common carrier railroad and the oldest railroad in the United States.

[2] Sandoval is approximately 65 miles east of St. Louis, Missouri.

[3] A homeless, orphaned, or abandoned child.

[4] Levi Sutton Meredith (1845–1898), according to his obituary, was nearly a lifelong resident of Marion County, Illinois, being both its surveyor and the town clerk of Salem.

ch. ends p. 15

the name of Harry Robinson, and told him my parents were dead. He questioned me at some length and finally offered me a home, which offer I accepted. In a week I was sick and for almost a week out of my head. To my knowledge it was the first time I'd ever had a doctor. I was living in their stable, and it was then I got sick and recovered. I lived there five weeks before the wanderlust overtook me. Mr. and Mrs. Meredith were away the day I left, and before going I emptied the pantry of a batch of gooseberry pies — there were seven large ones, freshly baked.

"I caught a freight and made Vincennes, Indiana,[5] the end of the division I was riding. It was early in the day, and on the outskirts of the quaint French town I saw a substantial brick house, where I applied for food. The lady of the place made me go to the stable, where she filled a half barrel with warm water and I took a bath — the freight of the night previous had been none too clean. After breakfast, and a good one, too, I went to sleep in the barn. About one o'clock a colored girl from the house awakened me and, giving me a tin pail, informed me that I was to go to the raspberry patch and pick berries. The pail I threw away, by way of thanks, and struck out along the tracks of the Terre Haute and Vincennes Railroad. It was very hot, and before I had gone far I fell in a faint on the tracks.

"Just ahead of me was a work train of twelve or fifteen flat cars heavily loaded with sand and railroad ties. In order to side-track for an express the engineer backed his train on top of me. The pain and shock as I was dragged along in the sand and cinders brought me back to consciousness and I screamed as men never heard mortal scream before. The brakebeam of the last car, which came on me first, caught my arm and clothing, and instead of being cut in two I was pushed and dragged along. My screams of agony were heard above the noise of the moving train and it was brought to a stop. Men hurried to the spot and lifted me out, torn and

---

[5] Vincennes, southwest of Indianapolis, is approximately 87 miles east of Odin.

bleeding. They put me on a sand car and backed into Vincennes, where I was removed to a hotel and laid out on a card table, where a doctor went over my hurts. Miraculous as it may seem, I was not seriously injured, although the flesh was badly torn from my right arm, both above and below the elbow. A carriage took me four miles outside the city to the poor farm, where I was admitted under the name of Harry Robinson. I am sure if any of the papers of that date remain on file, an account of the accident will be found. The story spread rapidly, and a score or more of people drove out the next week to see the boy who had been run over by a train and had lived to tell of it. In ten days I was able to be about again and ran away to the railroad, where I went blind baggage, and at Tunnelton, Ohio,[6] the crew found me all but blinded by the smoke and cinders. I was in mighty bad shape. They took me off and left me with some railroad men, who, taking pity on me because of my age, fixed me up and fed me up. In a short time I was able to travel. The men then gave me a pass on a passenger train to Cincinnati.

"I was sick again before I left the train, and, after two or three days of aimless roving about Cincinnati, I was desperately ill with malarial fever. Being a Catholic by birth I experienced no difficulty in securing admittance to a Sisters' Hospital. I've forgotten the name of the Institution, but for two months I lay there seriously ill. Finally when I became convalescent[7] they transferred me to a Catholic Protectory two or three miles outside the city. There a young student for the priesthood became interested in me and I spent a good deal of time in his company. Two or three times he took me to a show in the city. On one of these trips, in the meantime having become restless, I ran away from him and the institution. I remember how he begged me not to leave

---

[6]   Based on our research, we could find mentions of a Tunnelton, Ohio, but could not pinpoint its location as it does not exist today. It's also possible that he meant Tunnelton, Indiana, which lies approximately 75 miles east of Vincennes and 125 miles west of Cincinnati.

[7]   Recovering from an illness.

ch. ends next p.

him as an escape would count against him. His appeal was useless! He was a kind fellow, for he might have spoken to the policeman who stood near us, and who would have arrested me at once.

"You mustn't forget that all this time I was stealing everything I wanted from anyone I wanted to. I had become very expert with my hands. I could pick a door lock, open a locked window, extract a pocketbook or open a cash drawer with great skill and dexterity. Nothing frightened me, nothing stopped me, and yet I hadn't reached the age of twelve.

"Not liking Cincinnati, now that I had run away from the Protectory, I jumped a freight on the Panhandle and made Pittsburg. On leaving the railroad yards I braced[8] the first man I met and told him a hard luck story — a bunch of lies, of course. He proved easy, and took me to his house near an iron foundry, of which he was assistant superintendent. Frederick Jones was his name. I wonder if he is still alive? He did all for me that a father could have done. He clothed and fed me and insisted that I stay with him till I fully recovered from the effects of the fever. When I was again able to travel he took up a collection for me from among his friends, and with the money we bought a ticket to New York. That was the first time I'd ever paid for a fare on a railroad, and yet I'd ridden hundreds and hundreds of miles.

"Notwithstanding the fact that in those days a boy with a ready tongue could beg almost anything he wanted, I did comparatively little of it. It was too tame, it offered no excitement. I much preferred to steal, for that seemed to satisfy me. 'Canada Blackie,' that wonderful example of what 'love' can do for a bad man,[9] said, before his regeneration, that the greatest sensation he ever had in his life he experienced while he held a loaded revolver to the head of an engineer

---

[8] In this context: confront with requests.

[9] John E. Murphy, alias Canada Blackie, was known as New York State's most notorious criminal until he met Thomas Mott Osborne and saw Osborne's "new penology" in action. His story is told in *The Story of Canada Blackie* by Anne P. L. Field. Now available as a Heathen Edition!

and ordered him to stop the train.[10] I know what he meant, for even as a boy I experienced my greatest thrills in my most reckless and daring crimes.

---

[10] The actual line is: "The greatest sensation I ever had was standing with a loaded revolver over an engineer's heart, and ordering him to slow down an express train for *me!*" Found in the first chapter of *The Story of Canada Blackie.*

4.

In New York and in
Trouble in One Night

"On my very first night in New York I was picked up by a cop.
I was charged with a terrible crime — sleeping in a hallway!
The authorities didn't know, mind you, whether I was a good
boy or a bad boy, or whether I had ever been arrested before,
but they locked me in a cell all right. In the morning a chance
was given me to tell my story and I told it. I told them I was
an orphan with an aunt in Boston. They didn't know whether
I lied or told the truth. They made no effort to find out.

"Without notifying the Boston authorities that they were
sending them a young boy and to be on the lookout for him;
without waiting to learn whether I would shortly be reported
missing from some home in New York, a policeman took me
to the Fall River Line and shipped me east, like a barrel of
pork.

"Suppose your little boy should run away, and should later
reach the police. Suppose he was foolish enough or wicked
enough, call it whatever you will, to tell the police he lived in
Boston. Suppose the police did with him as they did with me.
Would you feel that such a system was a wise one? It makes a

vast difference, you know, whether a man thinks generalities or whether he brings the case right close home.

"In those days and in much later days, too, such occurrences were common. There was no reason other than custom for dealing with police cases. Everybody got the same sort of senseless treatment dictated by custom. And that method came right on down through the years unaltered, until recently such men as Judge Ben Lindsey of Denver began to use common sense and humane methods with results that have astonished a public long asleep, and have saved hundreds and hundreds of boys from leading lives of crime.[1] And now an era of common sense and humanity is dawning in our manner of administering prisons. For years we threw men into our prisons. And what did we release at the end of the term? Were they better or worse for the punishment? What chance had they to go straight? What does the average individual think of a man who has been branded as a criminal? Tell me!

---

[1] Benjamin Barr Lindsey (1869–1943) was known as the father of juvenile law. He established the first juvenile court in Denver, Colorado, and was known for his advocacy for juvenile rights, women's rights, and workers' rights.

5.
Doing My First "Bit"

"Boston proved easy. For about four months I lived high and indulged my every boyish fancy on the proceeds of my stealing. I tackled everything that came within my ken[1] and which looked at all promising. I knew no fear. Desire at once became determination — determination at once became action.

"One day I deliberately walked into a candy store, helped myself to the contents of the cash drawer and got away before the eyes of the astonished proprietress. But I had been too bold, too many had seen the trick and I was picked up, tried, and sent away.

"They took me first to the almshouse[2] at Tewkesbury, Massachusetts, a sort of detention station prior to delivery at a reform school. But they didn't know the boy they were handling, and as they made no effort to size me up they paid for their carelessness. On the third day I planned to escape and the next night made a clean 'getaway' and took five other lads with me. All these boys weakened once they got beyond

---

[1] One's range of knowledge, perception, or understanding.
[2] A poorhouse endowed by a public or private charity.

the walls and in a few hours all of them had returned and given themselves up to the authorities. Not me, however!

"Daredevil, reckless kid that I was, I at once returned to Boston and stole right and left under their very noses. Five weeks, or thereabouts, thus went on before they caught me, red handed, too, stealing fruit from a freight car.

"They were more careful in their handling of me this time and saw to it that I was safely landed at once in the State Primary School near Palmer, Massachusetts. Although it was about noon when I arrived, I had managed, quite easily by the way, to get into trouble by night, and then it was that I met Jimmy Lally, the hospital nurse.

"With the exception of one of the principal keepers of Sing Sing Prison, he was the most cruel and heartless man I ever knew. Each of them gloried in and thrived on misery and pain and discomfort in others and neither of them was ever known to allow an opportunity to go by uncanceled. Two men more wholly unfit for the jobs they held never lived. I know. I served under each. Under one as a boy. Under the other as a man. Who knows better than I know? Who could know better than I know? Each of these men secured his job through politics. Each man held his job through politics.

"Jimmy Lally looked at me. I wonder if he knew I was only 12 years old? I wonder if it would have made any difference if he had known? Two huge brass keys, each nearly a foot long, were suspended about his waist by a stout cord. And as he looked at me he slowly drew this cord in until the two big keys came into his hands. He held one in each fist.

"'Jack and Mick can play a trick,' he said.

"As he spoke the word 'Jack' he brought the key in his right hand down on the top of my head with a resounding blow and as he spoke the word 'Mick' the key in his left hand struck my head an even harder blow.

"The scalp had broken in two places and blood streamed down my face.

"This paid officer of the law was reforming me!

ch. ends next p.

"You know what hate does for a boy. You know what brutality does for a boy. I was no exception. I hated that man from that moment. At times I would have killed him had I found the chance. He was a big man and strong. At the time I met him he was about sixty years old. I wonder how many other boys' heads he busted? While I was there it was a frequent event, and he always prefaced the action with the same remark about 'Jack' and 'Mick.'

"Nor was he the only brute in charge of us. I was struck full in the face and knocked prostrate by a keeper's clenched fist many times. The assistant superintendent, a big, powerful fellow named Tibbetts, set the styles in discipline and as he had been, prior to his appointment at Palmer, a first mate on deep sea sailing vessels, you can imagine how kind, considerate and gentle a fellow he was to place in charge of boys with whom any results were wished for other than hardened, vicious characters.

"Tibbetts, like the large majority then and now, was a political office holder.

"I was always a rebel, mind you; always on the wrong side of everything. I needed discipline, and that badly. But everyday I stayed at Palmer the chances of my reforming were growing less and less. I possessed and used the faculty of causing more trouble in less time than any boy I ever knew or heard tell of. But each time I got beat up and came away bleeding I added a little more to my already large quota of viciousness. What could you expect if not that? I wasn't old enough to reason that anger and hate and viciousness would get me nowhere.

"After two visits to the dungeons or punishment cells I did learn to avoid those infractions of rules which meant 'downstairs.' It was too terrible. The dungeons and all they meant in that boys' school at Palmer were as terrible and as cruel as those for hardened burglars in San Quentin and Sing Sing in their palmiest days. Again, I know!

"Can you imagine the effect of such treatment on the

minds and morals of young boys? Thank God that the boys of today are being treated in a somewhat more humane manner. Thank God that correctional institutions are now making an effort to correct rather than to crush — to build up rather than to tear down. Thank God for such a woman as Mother Booth[3] and for such men as Thomas Mott Osborne, Dean Kirchway,[4] Canada Blackie, Jack Murphy,[5] Donald Lowrie,[6] and others of the new penology! A bright era has dawned and we've all got to keep it going!

---

[3] Catherine Booth (1829–1890), along with her husband William Booth, co-founded The Salvation Army and, because of her influence in its formation, was known as the "Mother of The Salvation Army."

[4] George W. Kirchway (1885–1942) was a professor of law at Columbia University for 25 years, and its dean for 10 years. He was appointed temporary acting warden of Sing Sing in January 1916 after mismanagement charges were made against then warden Thomas Mott Osborne.

[5] During Thomas Mott Osborne's one week of voluntary imprisonment at Auburn Prison, he developed the idea of what became the now legendary Mutual Welfare League during his daily conversations with Jack Murphy, Auburn No. 32177, as detailed in *Within Prison Walls*. Now available as a Heathen Edition!

[6] Donald Lowrie's first book, *My Life in Prison*, which details his 10 years spent as an inmate in San Quentin State Prison kick-started the American prison literature genre and instigated nationwide prison reforms still in effect today. Now available as a Heathen Edition!

6.

In Which I Am Bound Out

"After I had been at Palmer about a year, or possibly a little longer — after my body was covered with marks and bruises where they had beaten me black and blue to reform me and teach me what love meant, the great state bound me out to a German and his wife at East Hampton. This man, whose name I've forgotten, was the foreman in a suspender factory. As was then the custom I was to remain with him until I was twenty-one, during which time he was to care for me and give me a home. And I in turn was to learn his trade and answer to him in all ways. And so I went to work in his shop. It lasted longer than I had expected it would. A long five weeks went by before I decided that I had learned all I wanted to about the manufacture of suspenders. I made up my mind to beat it. How was I to do it? Instantly the answer came. I was at my bench at the time. I dropped what I was doing and went straight away to the grocer with whom the foreman traded. I told that grocer in a plain, simple manner that my boss had sent me to him to borrow ten dollars until that night. Of course the merchant was skeptical and refused to let me have the money. Instead of letting it go at that (as most boys would have done) I argued with him until he was finally sorry I hadn't asked him for twenty. He gave me the ten.

"I thanked him and left the store. Instead of walking in the direction of the shop where my boss was, I went in the opposite direction — down the railroad ties at that — with the ten dollars in my pocket and with the grocer looking at me in open-mouthed amazement. However, he wasn't long in reaching my boss with the story and they lost no time in getting a horse and buggy. They caught me, of course, and brought me back to town. That night after supper we took a second buggy ride and the big front doors of the State Primary School at Palmer closed with a bang at my back and I was again a prisoner.

"During the few weeks in which I had been away from the School, the Superintendent had gone and a new man had been appointed in his place. Mr. Bradford was a very different sort. He was kind, naturally. His being a relative of the then Lieutenant Governor of the State accounted no doubt for a man of his temperament being appointed to the School. During the Civil War he had served as a chaplain of a Massachusetts regiment, I believe.

"Very soon Mr. Bradford began to have serious trouble with me and my record was looked up more thoroughly than ever before. He decided that Palmer was not the sort of a place I required and so he had me transferred to the Home for Incorrigible Boys at Deer Island.

"At this place I came under Superintendent Blackstone. Here I found the food was quite a bit better than at Palmer, but outside of that I had stepped from the frying pan into the fire or even worse. It was an institution for incorrigibles! They said so themselves! They admitted that each inmate was a hopeless case, so why question it. Why try and find even *one soul* among them who wasn't? What was the use of trying to make them better boys? You wouldn't treat a dog one-half as badly as they treated us. You'd be afraid the dog would spring at you and tear you to pieces. And the dog would, too,

ch. ends p. 26

if it got the chance and no onlooker would blame the animal. They had the school at Palmer resembling a kindergarten by comparison. If you fell asleep in church you got three or four days in a dungeon on a scant measure of bread and water once in twenty-four hours. These dungeons were dark, damp holes in the cellar, without a bed or mattress. Sometimes you got a board to sleep on. There were no toilets, so we used the bucket system.

"If an instructor or a guard smashed you in the face and floored you and you happened to crawl to your feet sooner than was expected you got a second smash or a vicious kick. Then after that you lay still!

"I went through all this! I went through it at a time in my life when a boy's character is most easily swayed and bent and molded into something very difficult to change as year follows year.

"However, I had broken laws. I was a thief and I should be punished. The fact that I was only a young lad (as were all the inmates) didn't seem to make any difference as to the kind of punishment they handed out.

"Blackstone soon discovered that his brutal treatment had but one effect on me. It increased my viciousness and wickedness and so again I was bound out to serve a new master. This time it was to a young farmer whose name I can't recall. The exact location, too, I've forgotten, although I remember it was a small village on the border between Maine and New Hampshire.

"The night of my arrival he met me at the train, assumed responsibility for me and away we went. We sat up nearly all night in front of a big log fire and talked. He asked me a thousand and one questions about myself and about the jails I'd been in. He called them jails, but the state called them *reform schools*. I told him all he wanted to know and more. Without realizing it I frightened him so badly that when at last I went to bed he sat down and wrote the authorities at

Deer Island to come and get me, which they did — and so I didn't become a farmer.

"Back at Deer Island among the incorrigibles, myself one of them! Back in the dungeon! Unconscious on the floor — knocked there by a paid servant of the law! And me a young boy!

"They simply couldn't stand for me; that was all there was to it. They must get rid of me. This time they bound me over to Sanborn and Boardman Co., of Newburyport, Massachusetts, the owners of the good ship *Hiawatha*, a two-master[1] in the cod fishing industry plying[2] between Newburyport and Labrador.[3] For them I was to make one voyage and need not return to the Home at Deer Island.

"And so for the last time I left a Reformatory — re-form — a place where a boy's habits, character, and thoughts are supposed to be made over again — new and fresh and good.

"Perhaps they did try!

"Perhaps the fault was *all* mine!

"I knew little enough of good the first time I went to a Reformatory, but I knew everything that was wrong when I left my last one!

"When I was 46 years old after my last prison term I didn't know a bit more wrong than I had been taught or had gathered in Reform Schools. *I simply had had more experience, that's all.*

"When I stood, unashamed, before Judge Cowing[4] to receive a sentence that was to take me to Sing Sing Prison he said to me in effect, 'John Goode, your name had better have been John Bad. You've broken every trust ever laid on you. You were paid to uphold the law — you were a policeman,

---

[1] A ship having two masts.

[2] Traveling a regular route for commercial purposes.

[3] The continental region of Labrador is in the easternmost province of Canada.

[4] Rufus Billings Cowing Sr. (1840–1920) served as a New York City Judge for 28 years, presiding over several sensational criminal and political corruption cases, until his retirement in 1906 when he entered his son's private practice as a Wall Street attorney.

ch. ends next p.

and yet you've broken the law time and time again. You're a bad man; I wish I might give you a longer sentence. You deserve it.'

"Yes, he was right. But he didn't go far enough, that's all. He might, and I think he should, have told the crowd of morbid people who were eagerly listening that I had received my criminal education in reform schools: that I was a product of the then method of handling bad boys.

7.
On Board Ship — Bound Out

"The night before the schooner sailed I was delivered to the skipper and locked in a top floor room of his house with the grown daughter of the family on guard outside.

"I was to sail in the morning on that ship — that abiding place of the devil — that piece of hell! I figured anything was better than the place I had left, so I lay down and went to sleep!

"Never so long as I live will I forget the scene on the wharf at sailing time. I, alone, of all who sailed, walked aboard the vessel. Some crawled aboard, others were carried aboard and the rest were thrown aboard. Each man had a skinful[1] of booze. It had been their last night ashore for six months to come. As we were to be towed out of the harbor and sail up the coast light[2] there was no last minute loading or work to do and the men made the most of their time in the neighboring 'shock' houses.

"And thus we sailed! At the time it made no great impression on me because that's about all I'd ever seen. But now as I look back at it I sicken — positively sicken! You know

---

[1] An amount of alcohol sufficient to make one drunk.
[2] Less than or without a full load.

what the voyage must have been! You've seen both sides of life. Fourteen men with little to do on the run up, more than enough to do while fishing, and little to do on the run down. Away from civilization, away from booze — away from women — ungovernable tempers — vilest of tongues!

"I needn't tell you how I was mistreated and abused and struck. I won't tell you why I was kicked bodily down into the hold of that vessel among thousands of dead fish and the man who did it not knowing whether I was dead or alive and not caring! The point is I lived through it and in six months' time was back home. Home! What a word for me to use about myself.

"The skipper gave me an old sou-wester,[3] a pair of rubber boots, and two dollars and I had been paid! I was free!

"I need not go back to the reformatory for they were through with me. They had reformed me — the great State of Massachusetts virtually said so in releasing me. And, furthermore, had they not found a place for me where I could prove my fitness and prove myself a good boy? Had they not bound me out to the skipper of the good ship *Hiawatha*? Surely they had done enough! Had they not left my body covered with marks where they had beaten me to teach me the difference between right and wrong? What more could any reasonable boy expect? Yes, I was free! And so out again I went alone to face the world — to buck and beat the tides of fortune.

---

[3] A traditional collapsible and waterproof oilskin rain hat that is longer in the back than the front to protect the neck fully.

8.
In Which I Meet My Aunt

"The old desire to go to my mother's sister again came over me and at once I was on my way. Well do I remember arriving at her house and how shy I felt and how I hesitated about entering. Well do I remember how glad she was to see me, how she cried and hugged and kissed me on learning who the big, raw lad in front of her was.

"How strange it seemed! How awkward I felt! How I shrank from her caresses! It was more than I could understand. Other women and girls had kissed me. But not because they were glad to see me. Not because they had learned who I was. Why did she? I know now — she loved me — but I didn't know then.

"I had no more than arrived when I began to get uneasy. I remained with her only a few hours. The rooms seemed to suffocate me and the thought of remaining inactive and in such small quarters sickened me.

"At noon time my aunt put a good, big hot meal in front of me. It was then that I told her I must be going on my way. One of the fishermen had told me about Philadelphia and I had decided to go there. My aunt gave me five or six dollars, all she had in the house. As I was leaving I remember her looking at my feet and all that remained of the boots I was wearing tied to my feet with coarse string. She called me back and taking off her own shoes gave them to me and I was off!"

John Goode paused, arose from his chair and strode heavily up and down the room. Violent emotions surged through his huge frame. He stopped in front of his chair. I feared he had reached a point where he could go no further. I was about to speak — to change the subject — when he resumed his seat, and looking me full in the eyes, said:

"I remember I was tempted to go back to my aunt late that afternoon."

A far-away look settled over his face and I knew he was thinking of all the years he had lost — of all that might have been his had he but heeded the first good temptation he had ever known. After a while he regained his composure and resumed:

"I made Philadelphia on the trucks in four days. Part of my money I spent on clothing of which I was in sore need.

"What a strange thing it is how easily like meets like in this world ofttimes[1] with little or no effort. Immediately I ran into a gang of men who had boys stealing for them both in the city and on the road, and as I knew that well and nothing else I had no difficulty in securing a job and on the road I went.

"You probably wonder how it was that most of the people I met were thieves working gangs of boys. Wouldn't it have been stranger otherwise? I was riding freights mostly. Such men in those days made their headquarters in or near railroad yards and they were on the lookout for boys. I was a boy. They knew the type of lad I represented. I knew the type of man they represented. It didn't take long to get wise, for we didn't talk weather, politics, or foreign exploration.

[1] Often.

9.
Now a Professional Thief

"In exactly the same way that I beat my way east as an eleven-year-old boy I now retraced my steps and beat my way west as an experienced and expert thief. I can't tell you how it was that gambling got so strong a hold on me. I had always gambled even as a small boy, but the habit grew on me rapidly now as all evil habits do until all at once I realized that I was its slave — I was completely in its grip. So badly had I the habit that instead of stealing because stealing satisfied me, I found I was stealing in order that I might have means with which to satisfy my desire for chance — for the table, the cards, and the horses.

"By this time I must confess I knew fully the wrong in the life I was leading. I was now beyond fifteen and ignorance could excuse me no longer. My powers of observation were naturally keen and the training they had received had not dulled them any. I had suddenly realized that the side of the fence I had chosen for my path through life was the crooked one.

"I began to think about it. I began to wonder about people and about things. This was something I'd never done before. It proved mighty interesting. The people I thought about and the things I thought about were the only people and the only things I knew. I couldn't get outside of my environment and so I didn't change. And I know lots of people today who ought to get outside of their present environment but who can't.

"I knew the biggest gamblers between New York and Chicago and I frequented their places. I knew the most daring 'yeggmen'[1] — the most skillful 'dips'[2] — the whole profession in fact. And so when I began to think about people those were the people I thought about. I knew those people were doing dishonest and unlawful things and so when I began to think about things those were the things I thought about. Like thousands and thousands of other folks I did all my thinking along the lines of least resistance!

"Heretofore most of my stealing had been done because I needed something — food — clothes — fares or living necessities of one sort or another. Now, however, came the big change. I began to steal as a business, as a profession. And at fifteen then I had become a professional thief. That means one who realizes the wrong when he stops to think about it (which he never does), one who willingly and without duress accepts such work as a life task, as a means of accomplishing that which has domination over the mind. As the desire for gambling dominated all else in me I became a professional thief that I might gamble with the proceeds!

"What does it matter how many other times I was arrested for breaking the law or how many other prison terms I served? I've told you in detail my life to this point simply because these events took place when I was a boy. And an uneducated, untrained and naturally wild boy of eleven or thirteen or fifteen should not be expected to reason out successfully problems as big as my problems were. It isn't reasonable. As I look back at it all now I can excuse the result I had become

---

[1] Bank burglars who use nitroglycerine on safes, and prepare the compound themselves.

[2] Pickpockets.

at fifteen. From then on, however, I can't excuse it and I make no effort to do so.

"I want to pass over the next ten or fifteen years quickly but I want you to know them because I want you to know the sort of a creature I was when I first began to know what life really meant — to know what opportunities life gives us — to know the joy of being of use and of doing for others — to know the purpose for which God put me here.

"Yes, I went to prison again and again. The only reason I am not a murderer is because the bottle I used as a club was a full one and it broke when it smashed his skull. In prison I was punished again and again. And after an absence of about fifteen years New York again became my hangout.

"I had reached manhood and ten years more — physically, I mean. Mentally and morally I hadn't even begun. Each succeeding year my disposition had become meaner, dirtier, and blacker. My temper was a thing to dread and my size and strength coupled with it made a combination few men dared question.

10.

Getting in Right

"Society owed me a living, I reasoned out and I proceeded to collect it. Nothing good got even a look-in at my soul. I hated all men who were honest and I believed there were very few such. Everyone I knew was a grafter. My only desire was to gamble and I was cheap and dishonest even among my own kind.

"What thief and gambler is there who doesn't finally locate in New York to stay until it gets too warm for him? And so I came. The crowds of visitors, the excitement, the chance for easy money, all these things entranced and held me. Coney Island and its adjacent race tracks thrilled me. It goes without saying that I was a hard drinker — a drunk. For a long time I didn't use whiskey, but the day came. After repeated losses my nerves needed something to brace them and whiskey did the trick. Thousands of men start that way.

"I hadn't been here in New York long before I became acquainted with a bunch of cheap ward politicians — the hangers-on to those who governed your city. Thank God their kind is fast disappearing. Events of the past few years have either cleaned them out or compelled them to put on the soft pedal. Things began to come easier. My new friends, each a gambler and drinker, were wise and I lost no time in getting wise too!

"With friends like my new ones, politicians, I became more daring, more reckless. It was easy to avoid trouble, for influence was bought and sold like any of the household commodities you are familiar with. Protection was an article of merchandise like coal or like stocks. The price fluctuated with the conditions. Sometimes it was cheap — sometimes expensive, but it could always be had. Sometimes it was bought with cash, sometimes with cigars, whiskey, and women, and at other times with personal service.

"I became a part of that side of New York. I aligned myself with the lowest and most despicable end of society and I did it all with a full knowledge of what it meant.

"It was about this time that women became a factor in my life. Women figured largely in the new circle of friends among whom I was now traveling. I mean women — not wives!"

11.
In Which I Marry

"About this time I learned of a woman who was employed in the rectory[1] of one of New York's swellest churches on a street in the Twenties. This woman had a bank roll of about two thousand dollars, the hard-earned savings of many years of toil. To me that sounded good. With two thousand dollars I could make a killing at the track. The more I thought about that two thousand the more I wanted it. The more I thought about owning it the more I thought about owning the owner of that two thousand also. I laid a wager I'd get her.

"It was time I married. All my friends, the cheap politicians, were married. There were times in the life we were leading when it was a good thing to be known as being married. When it wasn't necessary as a sort of protection they didn't care whether anyone knew they were married or not. And then again, a home and a wife were handy, convenient things when one wanted to sleep off a drunk or when one wanted a game of poker. It would be convenient for me to have a wife now and so I promptly set out to get one.

"Did I love this woman? No, I did not. I couldn't for the

---

[1] A residence provided by a church for its parson or vicar or rector; parsonage.

life of me have told what it meant to love. And so I deceived this good, pure woman that I might make her my wife, secure her savings and then treat her as fancy dictated, keep her or throw her over. I covered up my past. That was easy for she believed in me. I associated myself with her church and through her I was made its janitor. It's hard for a man to believe that anyone could be as yellow as I was with that woman. But the fact remains that I was. I married before she even suspected that I drank. Here I was, a lying, drinking, gambling, thieving man, a Catholic janitor of a Protestant Church and the husband of as pure and innocent a woman as ever lived.

"It's hard to tell a story like this, but it's the truth! That's the thing I had become! That's what years of sin made me — that's what sin will make of anyone if given time. Not only because it's true do I want to tell it but because through seventeen years of the same treatment, yes and worse treatment, that true and brave and loyal little woman stood by me and her marriage vows — for better or for worse, they had been!

"The two thousand was easily obtained and went as easily just as planned. Then we were busted. And so again I went to stealing for I had to drink and I had to gamble and that required more money than the church paid me.

"We were now in a little place of our own, she in the meantime having left her duties in the rectory. The women of the parish, many of them very wealthy, loved my wife and some of them visited her in our little home. I met them both at home and at the church, and I acknowledged their love and their many kindnesses to my wife by helping myself to those of their belongings which pleased my fancy.

"Sometimes I came home to her regularly. Sometimes for days and weeks at a time she didn't know whether I was dead or alive.

"But she prayed!

"She prayed for me till the day she passed away.

ch. ends next p.

"God answers prayer. He answered hers. That's my greatest comfort now!

"And then came a time when she, penniless and alone, was forced to go out and earn her own living. She could get nothing from me and she was too proud to ask for aid at the only other place where she might have expected to find it and where she would have found it. And thus things went on! More and more of the time I was away and one after another of her friends dropped their calling. She would not give *me* up so they were forced to give *us* up.

"When I needed money quickly, which happened frequently, I'd take all she had — steal her paltry earnings — clean her out of everything of value. Time after time this happened and still she stuck, wishing, hoping, begging, crying, praying that I would change.

"And me? Yes, I promised! I'd promise anything for money!

"That then was the sort of husband I made her.

"There are men today doing the same things. I want them to know my story — to know that no matter how far down a fellow gets there's a sure road up — a sure road to happiness for them and for their wives!

12.

In Which I Begin to Slide Downhill From Which There is But One Path Back

"The New York pace in the underworld to which I belonged was a pretty stiff one. It required great nerve force to keep it up. A man needs stimulation in order to stand it long. The life keeps a man up day and night. I was no exception and I needed stimulation. Like all in my class I thought whiskey gave it to me. Before long I was either drunk or half drunk day and night. And then my skill as a thief began, little by little, to disappear. I bungled things that I used to get away with easily. My nerve had gone too.

The sharp, keen edge of my wits had become dulled by drink. The days of easy money were gone. It was harder and harder to get. And then came a time when I was forced to go to my friends, the politicians, and ask for a job.

"There was still enough of me left intact so that at times I could be of use to them and I got the job. They made me a foreman in the Street Cleaning Department. What a fine specimen of a man to be working for the city! What a type to put in charge of their workmen. However, I was part of a rotten political bunch and I was taken care of just as others, before and after me, were cared for.

"There on the department things eased up a bit. There was considerable to be had in the way of graft and I wasn't long in getting wise. To most of it, I had been tipped off in advance. The rest I dug up and developed myself. The biggest cleanup came from the snow.

"My wife got none of my money, not even my salary. I gambled it all away long before I received it. She was earning what she could in a bitter fight to clothe and feed herself and pay the rent.

"I pulled myself together temporarily after I had been on the Street Cleaning Department about three years. I went a step higher through the same politicians.

"All my life, mind you, I had broken the law — the law of every state and city I'd ever visited. *Law* was nothing to me. Those who were paid to uphold the law were nothing to me except grafters. I didn't believe there was an honest policeman in the world. Everyone I had known was crooked. Understand me, please, I don't want to cast any suspicion on policemen as a group. I am telling only what I know from personal experience. All of my intimate friends among them and among those who in any way contributed to the conduct of the great city of New York were crooks or grafters in a small or big way, depending only on opportunity.

"Despite my record and my principles, well known to all who were instrumental in securing my appointment, I was made a member of the city police force in June of 1900. There, of course, I had all sorts of opportunity for inside information on the ponies. I knew all the poolrooms and all the bookmakers. In addition there were always crooks and gamblers anxious to stand in with the cops and thus I was always getting good tips.

"Never in my life had I gambled so recklessly. I could think of nothing else and did nothing else. In all the time I was on the force I didn't do one honest day's work. I didn't have to. I was in right at first and after that I didn't know or care what I did for I was nearly dead from drink and all else that went with the life I was leading.

"It was while on the force and in my uniform too that I escaped being a murderer by the smallest possible margin. I had left my beat to get a drink at a joint which was being run by the mistress of a man well up in city affairs. The place was a favorite hangout for members of the force, officers as well as patrolmen. I was drunk at the time. An Italian stood at the bar. We had never seen one another before. He misunderstood a drunken jeer I made to a friend and he called me a name not even a low-down thief would tolerate. Blind with rage I picked up a full bottle of soda, raised it high above my head and brought it down on the top of his skull with all my strength. Again the politicians! They sent me into retirement for three days while the affair was hushed up. The man didn't die, although it was five weeks before the doctors would admit that he could live. On the fourth day I returned to my post. Fifty dollars' worth of cigars and liquors squared off my indebtedness to the gang who had covered up for me!

"Another man than yourself, one not familiar with the human dregs who populate certain sections of New York, would not admit that I could go any lower down the social scale. But I was a long way from the bottom still!

"Before long the day came when even my friends, the politicians, could not longer afford to cover my tracks — to back me up in the front office. Shortly thereafter I was transferred to a precinct on Staten Island. There I went gambling without restraint. My nerves broke completely in two for the first time. I was heavily in debt. My courage was gone and I was on the verge of D. T.'s;[1] I hadn't a cent. My room rent was due and the landlord was insisting on payment. Had I

---

[1] Delerium Tremens: A psychotic condition and withdrawal syndrome occurring in persons who have developed chronic alcoholism, characterized by tremors, hallucinations, anxiety, and disorientation.

ch. ends next p.

been able to go to New York I would have stolen or borrowed the few necessary dollars from my wife.

"As I left the station house that night I raised[2] a twenty-five cent loan and bought a vial of poison — for a dog I told the druggist — but in reality it was for something far worse than a dog. I was through with it all and had decided to go the 'Dutch route.'[3] I wrote a couple of letters, sealed them, and then locked the door to my room from the inside. I thought I was a man. I didn't know how big a coward I was. I removed my coat, vest, trousers, shirt, and shoes and stood in my underwear with a big flask of whiskey in one hand and the vial of acid in the other. Try as I would I couldn't muster sufficient courage to drink the stuff. A dozen times the vial got almost to my lips but no further. Not so the whiskey, however, and I finally fell to the floor in a dead, drunken stupor. In the morning I threw the poison down a sink. That debauch lasted about three days for I made a killing early that day in a poolroom and cashed in about twenty.

"When I finally returned to my station house I found serious charges, which I could not successfully beat, had been preferred against me. I removed my shield, unbuckled my belt, and turned in my gun and stick. I had beaten a dismissal by only a few days!

---

[2] Obtained; acquired.
[3] A slang term, also known as the "Dutch act," which means to commit suicide.

13.
My Last Prison Term

"Back in New York again and without money, without pull, without friends. No, that was not so! I knew there was one who was still my friend, my wife! She had moved and I had some little difficulty in locating her. Then I found that one of her former loyal friends, a member of her old church, was again in touch with her.

"Jane was glad to see me — she cried and implored me to stay with her and to behave myself. This, of course, I readily agreed to do and I did so until she got together a few spare dollars and then I left and took the money with me. I did not see her again until I was sentenced to six years at hard labor in Sing Sing Prison by Judge Cowing.

"With the few dollars she gave me I got beastly drunk. I met an old acquaintance who tipped me off to a good thing. I needed money quickly if I was to make use of this information. A car soon brought me to the home of my wife's old friend, this woman who was again befriending her. On other occasions I had stolen from her, but because of her friendship for Jane she had refused to prosecute me.

I entered her house and stole an expensive silver service.[1] I was caught, tried, convicted, sentenced, and away I went, with my wife promising me her continued love and support and begging me to turn over a new leaf. Again I promised her I would.

"I was an interesting and strange creature as with nineteen others I was taken over the New York Central to Sing Sing to serve my last 'bit.' The fact that I was going to 'stir' didn't disturb me. I felt no shame or remorse over that. Nor did I regret the act for which I had been sent away. My friends had deserted me, the old 'pull,' which had safeguarded me so many times, had been withdrawn, and I was sore. I wanted to get even.

"One by one the big events in my life passed in review before my eyes. I saw my mother and my father. I saw the Judge who drove me out of St. Louis as a boy. I saw Jimmy Lally and the 'screws'[2] and keepers who had mauled and beaten me in all the different places where I had done time. And then I saw my wife in her poverty and anguish of heart. So far as any effect was concerned I might as well have been thinking of the moon or the stars. All emotion, all feeling of right, all honor, were buried in me. Buried under years of dissipation and sin, buried so completely that I was as vicious and heartless a man as ever lived.

"Life in the various 'stirs' I had been in taught me one thing well — to obey rules. Not because they were rules or because it was right to obey rules, but because the powers that made them had sticks loaded at the end with lead, and guns and pistols and solitary punishment cells and the power to deprive me of food and water and all I had was a pair of bare fists. And bare fists against a dozen armed 'screws' didn't stack up good. As a rule prison authorities have no trouble with second, third, and fourth termers. They're wise! Their spirit has been broken. It's only the new fellows, the

[1] A complete set of silverware.

[2] Slang for turnkeys or jailers, the persons in charge of the keys of a prison.

At a Court of General Sessions of the Peace

of the City and County of New York, holden in and for the County of New York, at the Building for Criminal Courts in the Borough of Manhattan of the said City on *Mon* day, the 22nd day of *January*, in the year of our Lord one thousand nine hundred and *Six*

PRESENT,

The Honorable RUFUS B. COWING,
City Judge of The City of New York,
Justice.

THE PEOPLE OF THE STATE OF NEW YORK

against

John G. Goode

On conviction by *Confession of Grand Larceny in the Second Degree*

Whereupon it is ORDERED and ADJUDGED by the Court that the said

John G. Goode

for the felony aforesaid, whereof he is convicted, be imprisoned in the STATE PRISON, at hard labor, for the term, the minimum of which shall not be less than *One (1)* year *and Six (6)* months, and the maximum of which shall not be more than *Four (4)* years *and Six (6) months.*

A true Extract from the Minutes.

Edward R. Carroll Clerk of Court

Facsimile of Commitment Papers Sending John Goode to Sing Sing

Statement of Commitments to the SING SING STATE PRISON, during the month of *January* 1906.

No.	NAME OF CONVICT	COUNTY	CRIME	COURT	JUDGE	DATE OF SENTENCE	RECEIVED AT PRISON	TERM Years	Months	Days	Fine
31	John G. Goode	New York	G. L. 2d	Elders	Cowing	Jan 22 1906	Jan 26 1906	4	6	—	—

[handwritten record]

1906
January 26

No. 56097

John T. Goode 7849

Received from *New York*   Court. *Gen Sessions*

Sentenced, *Jan 22 06; 4 6 Cow G L 2d*   *Cowing* Judge,

Who arrested you? ——————   Precinct No. *E 22 2nd of R Patrin*

Born *Boston Mass* Age, *39 looks older.*   Occupation, *Policeman & motorman*

Complexion, *Light* Eyes, *Hazel*   Hair, *Bro & gray*

Stature, *5 – 8½* Weight, *225*   Read *Yes* Write *Yes*

Habits, *Mod* Tobacco *No*   Religion, *Prot* Married or Single

Resided when Arrested, at *153 Bowery N.Y.C.*

Names of Relatives or Friends. *Wife Jane Goode 9 Gramercy Park N.Y.C. Rounded head 7 hat no 9 shoes. Head free from scars but on top both sides the scalp is in ridges, Forehead Rather narrow. Med Ears. Arched and med brows Short thick nose. Teeth very Poor mostly absent. Has lower false ones. Heavy Chin Large full face, Small mole near or Temple Scar from cut between 3r T.d finger The index finger Crippled*

1906   John G. Goode   7849

January 26 RECEIVED FROM New York   COURT. Gen. Sessions

No. 56097 SENTENCED, Jan. 22–06 Cow G. L. 2d   Cowing JUDGE,

WHO ARRESTED YOU? —————— PRECINCT No. E 22

BORN, Boston, Mass.   AGE, 39 looks older   OCCUPATION, Policeman & Motorman

COMPLEXION, Light   EYES, Hazel   HAIR, Brown and gray.

STATURE, 5–8½   WEIGHT, 225   READ, Yes   WRITE, Yes

HABITS, Mod   TOBACCO, No   RELIGION, Prot   MARRIED OR SINGLE,

RESIDED WHEN ARRESTED, AT 153 Bowery N.Y.C.

Names of Relatives or Friends Wife Jane Goode 9 Gramercy Park N.Y.C.
Rounded head — 7 hat, w 9 shoes.
Head free from scars but
on top both sides the scalp is in
ridges. Forehead rather narrow. Med
ears. Arched and med. brows. Short
thick nose. Teeth very poor
mostly absent. Has lower false ones.
Heavy chin. Large full face. Small mole
near   temple. Scar from cut between
      finger. The index finger crippled.

men with spirit and blood, full of life and fight, that cause trouble in prisons! And instead of taking that spirit and blood and fight and turning it in the right direction they kill it — grind it out of a man, crush his very soul, make him detest himself for being alive and make him hate with a fury that would kill if it got the chance. And then those men are turned loose and expected to go straight — expected to be good!

"During the whole of my stay I locked on 'The Flats.' That's the ground floor of the cell house. It's only eighty-two years old and it's only been condemned about eight times. For eighty-two years human beings have been thrown into 'The Flats' where the larger majority, myself one of them, contracted rheumatism.[3] Don't blame the authorities, blame the cell house. The authorities wouldn't give us toilets so why should they give us rheumatism? Be reasonable, man! The whole system of caring for us was worse than disgraceful — it was barbaric. We were locked in dirty, filthy, vermin-filled cells late Saturday afternoon. We were kept there all night, all day Sunday, all Sunday night, and when the Monday was a holiday we had a 'double header,' as we called it, and were released on Tuesday at 6 a.m. It's impossible for you or anyone else who hasn't done a 'stretch' like that to realize what it means. We came out with nerves on edge, ready to fight at anything — ready to tear a man to pieces at the slightest provocation.

"I got along fairly well because I behaved myself. Being an ex-cop, I was accepted only by a choice few as being all okay. Prisoners, as a class, have a motto, 'Once a cop, always a cop.' We even made 'book'[4] in the cart-and-wagon shop where I worked. One of the 'screws' had a 'runner'[5] who kept me informed as to what horses had already won their races, and then we opened up and did a swell business. I had

---

[3] Any disorder or disease marked by inflammation, pain, and stiffness in the joints, muscles, or connective tissue, especially rheumatoid arthritis.

[4] To "make book" is to take bets and give odds; gambling.

[5] A messenger or informer.

ch. ends next p.

been a stealing, grafting cop — had known other grafting cops — had seen politicians get rich on graft — knew judges who were grafters — had never known even one lawyer who wasn't a grafter, and here on the inside were prison attendants, lots of them, grafting on the inmates. Do you wonder that convicts as a class doubt society is on the level with them?

"The public is pretty well informed as to what Sing Sing was in those days. Mr. Osborne has taken care of that. I'd seen lots of filth and rottenness in my day but I'd seen nothing to touch what I found there. The cell house was alive — literally — with vermin. The stench from those hundreds and hundreds of buckets was awful at all times, and in the heat of summer was almost unbearable — it made my eyes feel like they were afire. The food and the tin plates we ate from were rotten. You'll wonder perhaps how *anything* could make me less of a man than I was, but the conditions I've mentioned did do that as they did in the case of every man who lived under them. Such a result was inevitable.

"The days and weeks and months dragged by and then a year, and another long year started in just the same way. We were rotting. There was not anywhere near enough work to keep us busy and so we rotted in those 3½ x 6 x 7-foot holes in that pile of granite put there eighty-two years ago for men to suffer in, that their evil ways might be made good ways. What a chance! Finally the day drew near when I could appear before the Parole Board. Mrs. Booth, the 'Little Mother' as she is affectionately called by thousands of 'cons' and 'excons,' came regularly to the prison. I attended her services simply because I could get out of my cell for a short time. And then one day I spoke to her and she offered to help me secure my release provided I would do as I should have done long ago. Like I had done hundreds and hundreds of times before, I made a promise on my honor to reform and serve God from then on.

"And so Mrs. Booth secured my release after a stubborn fight before the Parole Board.

"Was I thankful and grateful? Yes, just long enough to get clear of the joint —that's all. The 'Little Mother' sent me to Hope Hall where so many of her boys have come to realize what right means and how good it feels to be right — where so many of her boys have found God.

"Like a low-down cur I skipped in a couple of weeks and landed down and out in New York, but this time in a new section — the Bowery.

"Each month, in my report to the Parole Officer, I lied. It was easy to put it over — what did they care?

14.
At the Bottom of the Bottom

"Just as there is but one New York and one Paris and one Venice, so there is but one Bowery! There's no other street in the world like it that I know of. It's peopled with the dregs of humanity from the four corners of the globe — good and bad men, but all of them down and out. Down so far that not many of them ever get back. Down so low that there's just one of two things left to do — get up or die.

"The cheap, dirty lodging houses are packed to the doors nightly with these poor fellows, some of whom are there reaping the harvest of their own sowing while others there are the cruel victims of circumstances over which they had little or no control.

"The thief, the 'dip,' the 'yegg,' the 'con,' the black sheep of the well-to-do family, the green-goods man,[1] all of them are there, too old or broken to longer carry on their shady trades. The sick men, young and old, good and bad, they are there too, roaming about, eating and sleeping when and where they can, hoping against hope that the next moment may be their last. The bum is there too, living but never working,

---

[1] One who sold counterfeit money as "real" money allegedly made from authentic engraving plates stolen from the government.

and he's there in goodly numbers. By far the greatest number though are there because of their inability or unwillingness to desert the ranks of Old King Booze. You can't call it alcohol, it's anything but that. Those fellows can't get a 'kick' out of good whiskey and many of them can't get one out of 'third rail.'[2] What a life!

"There's still another class there and Heaven forbid that it should continue. It's the young class composed of boys who have been unable to resist the call to come to the great city, expecting to find plenty of helping hands and lots of work. Who is there, tell me, to take these boys by the hand? They wind up, after the small purse is gone, on the Bowery.

"Among that motley frightful population I fitted into a waiting place. They are always waiting for newcomers down there and they don't have to wait long either — that's the greatest pity of it all — they come faster than they go. Thus the great change that has taken place in the last few years is accounted for. There was a time when real 'bad men' haunted the Bowery and there pulled down their drag. Not so today, for the hard men and the gangs have gone east or west and some north, and left the old street exclusively for the men nearly through — for the man who has failed.

"Failed! Yes, that's it — the Bowery might well be called the Street of Failures!

"Was I a failure? I wouldn't have admitted it then. I'd soon be back up town. I remember I figured it out that way.

"While I had been doing my 'bit' up the river I had worked out an elaborate system to beat the ponies and had figured that with $1,537 I could beat the bookmakers to a crisp. Anyone would think that I'd been up against them often enough to know that in the long run they always held the trump card and couldn't be beaten. It takes a long time to teach some people, doesn't it?

"It seemed as though it ought to be very easy to get

---

[2] Incredibly strong alcohol.

ch. ends next p.

$1,500.[3] In the old days I could have done it, maybe in a day, certainly in a week. But on the Bowery it might take two weeks, I figured. So at it I went. The pickin' was poor, my pep had gone and the 'rot-gut' I'd been drinking for whiskey had taken all the flexibility out of both fingers and brain. 'Suckers' were few and far between and when you did get one a 'ten spot'[4] was a big haul. I never really knew how many Ingersoll watches there were until I saw the Bowery worked.[5] I never got the fifteen hundred or anything like it.

"A night or two ago as I walked up that old sin-soaked sidewalk I passed a party of shimmers — men in evening clothes attending an equal number of expensively dressed women. It gave me a start, for do you know the feeling a party like that arouses in the hearts of the poor devils that invest the dives down there?

"I'll tell you! Picture a back room of a saloon carpeted with dirty sawdust two inches deep, spotted here and there with filthy spittoons full and overflowing. One or two yellow gas flames vainly trying to fight a room full of foul, smoke-laden air. Imagine a dozen to two dozen half-dead, half-fed, half-mad, half-clad men lolling and lying around in cheap rickety chairs. Some are dead drunk, some are fighting drunk, while the remainder would like to be drunk only they haven't the price. And then somehow, by means of a never-failing underground system of communication, comes the single word 'Slummers'!

"The swells march in, a merry, laughing crowd, trying hard to act as though they were quite accustomed to it all. They are more careful about ordering drinks than they need be. They are served the best in the house and the boss sees

---

[3] Adjusted for inflation, $1500 in 1906 would be equivalent to approximately $50,000 in 2023.

[4] Ten dollars.

[5] The Ingersoll Watch Company grew out of a mail order business started in New York City in 1882 by brothers Robert Hawley and Charles Henry Ingersoll. In 1896, they introduced the Yankee, also known as the "dollar watch," which was the cheapest watch available at the time and the first to be priced at one dollar.

it reaches them 'right.' No petering a lot of drinks like that; it would mean too big a fuss.

"Some one of the men pulls out a bunch of yellow stuff, settles for the round, and passes the waiter a good fat tip.

"In that roll that's flashed there's often more money than some of the poor devils in the room have seen in a year. Those not too drunk to comprehend, grip the tables in front of them while beads of perspiration form in the hollows of their hands. Their eyes light up with anger, resentment, and hate. But no further sign is given. An attempt to pull anything off on a bunch like that would mean serious trouble 'downtown.' It's better to wait till they leave the joint and the men separate into ones and twos after leaving the women.

"I've felt all this many times. I remember one party in particular headed by a fresh young guy who thought he knew it all. He began by ordering, in a loud voice, a round for the house. He flashed too big a roll! Next morning we read in the papers of a young fellow answering his description, having been found uptown in a hallway cleaned out completely and still in a stupor. He never knew who did it, nor did I.

"Slumming is not dangerous business now, but it's dirty business though. If those people who practice it only knew the temptations they stir up and the sad and bitter memories they quicken in those poor fellows they would keep away or approach the problem in a more serious frame of mind.

15.
Just Before I Turned!

"I found a wholly new kind of work on the Bowery — the lowest down and dirtiest occupation it is possible to undertake. It just suited me and the low-tide condition of manhood I was in. A thief or a 'yegg' couldn't be bought to do it. Most 'bums' would turn up their noses at it and yet it was good pay. It was strike breaking — scab stuff — and the conditions under which it was done and the way we were handled would sicken a pig. But it didn't sicken me. I liked it! Nobody with any sense would ask a real man to do it — they looked up fellows like myself, and we were not a few. It didn't require no much urging to make me join the Pinkertons[1] and go out strikebreaking. My first job was at the big strike in Philadelphia.[2]

The drunker we got the less we cared how dangerous was the situation and the better our bosses liked it. So they gave

---

[1] Still in operation today, Pinkerton is a private security guard and detective agency established circa 1850 in the United States by Allan Pinkerton (1819–1884) and Edward Rucker (1822–1872). At the height of its power, Pinkerton was the largest private law enforcement organization in the world.

[2] The General Strike of 1910 was a labor strike by trolley workers of the Philadelphia Rapid Transit Company that grew to a citywide riot and general strike in Philadelphia, Pennsylvania.

us all the stuff we wanted. We had quantities of it in the car barns and on the cars themselves. Any time at all, anywhere, we were ready to fight to a finish without the slightest urging. That was part of the game and was what we were brought down to do, and so long as there was any strike left there was plenty of booze left.

"After things had quieted down sufficiently we would be paid, and well too, and then escorted to the railroad in a bunch and sent back to New York. It would never do for Philadelphia to have us turned loose there and it would go badly with each one of us individually if we stayed.

"I always got back from a trip like that with a good-sized roll and so long as it lasted I was busy day and night drinking and gambling — a never-ending succession.

"McGuirk's Suicide Hall,[3] The Alligator,[4] and Nick Solomon's,[5] beside a dozen others, became my hangouts. They were the hardest and lowest down dives in the city and I was probably the hardest and lowest down man in the city — again like met like!

"It was dangerous business for a stranger to show a bill in any one of those dumps. I've 'rolled' men for as little as a dollar. When a man's been 'rolled' he's been cleaned out of everything convertible quickly into booze and then thrown out the side door into the gutter, probably to be picked up by a cop and arrested for intoxication.

"I wonder how much the public knows about those dives. Very, very little I fear. At the time of which I speak the authorities knew all about them. After a big haul the thieves

---

[3] Irish immigrant John McGurk, who owned several saloons in the Bowery area of New York City (all of which were shut down by police), opened McGurk's Saloon in 1895 at 295 Bowery, between Houston and East 1st Street, and it quickly became known as one of the most notorious dive bars in New York. Then in 1899, there were reportedly six deaths and seven failed suicide attempts at the bar, which led McGurk to the macabre idea of capitalizing on his bar's newfound reputation by dubbing it McGurk's Suicide Hall until it was shut down in 1902.

[4] The Alligator Cafe, located at 263 Bowery, was a five-cent-a-shot joint operated by a former London surgeon known as "Doc" Shuffield.

[5] Nick Solomon's saloon, known for its "third rail," was located on Mulberry Street, which runs parallel with Bowery.

ch. ends next p.

would return to these dumps and then divide up with the representatives of the law who had been tipped off and who had shut their eyes and closed their mouths!

"I wonder if you realize how they chase a man's coin? I wonder if you know what little chance a man has of coming out of one of those places with so much as a nickel left? After one o'clock in the morning they used to let us sleep all night in the back room if we had the price of a drink left. And the stuff came then, two hookers[6] to the nickel. You hadn't a chance in the world of holding back a dime for a 'pad.' Many and many a man is forced to 'carry the banner,' that is, walk the streets all night. They can't hold back the price of a 'pad,' or even a nickel for two of those early morning drinks, with the privilege of sleeping in the back room.

"When it wasn't too cold it was much more desirable to 'carry the banner' than to sleep on a 'pad' in those rotten, foul smelling ten-cent lodging houses which line the Bowery for blocks. They are breeding places of crime, vermin, and disease. They are everything they should not be and not one single thing they should be.

"There's big money in it — the way those houses are run. Why doesn't some wealthy man or group of men equip a ten-cent lodging house with room say for five hundred men? Keep it clean and restrict it rigidly to men not drunk. Provide showers with hot and cold water. I'd guarantee to keep it full all the time with honest, sober, deserving men, men who would make good if they could find a place where they could sleep clean, and where they would be out of drink's temptation. I know of many cases where men who are 'off the stuff' and putting up a good fight have been awakened by someone in a nearby bunk inviting them to have a drink from an outstretched bottle. What chance has a fellow of quitting the stuff when he is reduced to living in joints of that caliber?

"The right kind of a house could be run for ten cents per 'pad' and no one would lose a penny — they might even make

[6] In this context, a hooker is a glass of undiluted alcohol.

a little! There certainly must be men, ten of them, who would be willing to form a company and subscribe, say twenty-five thousand dollars each, for a purpose like that! It's the biggest need the Bowery has to back up and make more effective the rescue work now going on there.

"Where are these men? Who are they? Tell me!

"How many of your friends or the general public realize that there are fully thirty thousand men in New York City who, though honest and willing to work, can't earn more than seventy-five cents a day? Most of these men are downtown and the problem they present is a difficult one to solve.

16.

In Which I First Visit the Bowery Mission

"After one of these strike-breaking jobs which had netted me a considerable sum of money, I returned to New York and began to spend it. It proved to be my most fearful debauch. It lasted for many days during all of which time I was a 'good fellow.' If you've got a dollar to spend you're a good fellow down there but when you've got a 'roll to blow' you meet scores of 'friends' you've never seen before. They come and go with the 'roll' like wolves with the stray sheep. I came to my senses finally, alone and penniless, in a back alley-way. I had a hazy feeling that I hadn't spent or gambled all the money I'd started in with the night before. I was sick, too, which added to my suspicions that my 'roll' had been 'lifted.' Someone had reached me!

"A man in the condition I was in that morning needs, if ever he needs it, a good stiff drink. It quiets him and if he can't get it he is liable to go clean crazy. Men like that are given a drink and at longer and longer intervals other drinks. Otherwise they would injure themselves or others. Somebody gave me a 'hooker.' It pulled me together a bit. And then a bartender where I had dropped a 'bunch' a few nights earlier gave me another.

"Suddenly I thought of my wife and then I remembered that I hadn't paid her a visit in a long time. Probably she had a few dollars saved. I needed money badly. What was my wife for, if not to take care of me? So I looked her up.

She was in desperate straits. Ill from worry and lack of proper food and days and days of fruitless searching for work — for any sort of work that would bring the price of a loaf of bread and a bottle of milk.

"Did my heart melt? Did I get down on my knees and ask forgiveness?

"In a moment of madness, after learning that she had no money to give me, I left her without so much as a goodbye!

"How I got back to the Bowery I don't know. I was blind with rage and the effects of booze — sore clear through with anger and hate. I hated myself. I hated my wife. I hated the world. I must have money! I must have money! This kept ringing in my ears!

"And then I lay down and slept. It was a long time before I awoke and when I did I found myself in an empty wagon in an alley.

"I was sober now — sober but sick. Not too sick, however, to begin new plans for money — money for drink, money for gambling. If I could pick one winner I could get a start and with a start, even if it was only a small one, I could beat the bookmakers. I knew it! I was surer of it then than ever before.

"I thought and planned with wits born of desperation, for somehow or other I felt this was pretty near my last fling. But I couldn't arrive anywhere. I couldn't see a start. I thought and thought but only in circles! I couldn't do anything alone. Alone? Why need I try alone? Hadn't I a wife? What was a wife for if not to help me and care for me? Hadn't she always done it? Wouldn't she continue to do it? I knew her well enough to know she would!

"I don't know what put the idea of writing to her in my

mind. But that's what I decided to do. I hadn't done it, mind
you, in years. I had no writing materials nor a stamp. It was
early in the morning and I could borrow what I needed,
maybe, from a bartender, so off I went. On the way I met
an acquaintance and told him what I wanted. He couldn't
help me himself but he told me that if I would go up to the
Bowery Mission, up near Rivington Street, and tell them I
wanted to write to my wife — that I wanted to go home and
be good to her again — they would give me the materials
and a place at which to write.

"I turned in my tracks and headed for the Bowery Mission.

"I want you to get clearly in mind the mental state I was
in and the purpose of my errand. I was on my way again to
make my poor wife 'produce.' Remember my physical condition — it had been wrecked by booze and wrong living. I was
a scoffer and a jeerer at everything that savored of religion.
I didn't believe there was a square man in the world. I would
have thought no more of killing a man than of laughing
at one. In reform schools and prisons I had been told of
brotherly love one hour a week by a paid chaplain, while I
was being beaten on my bare back, strung up by my thumbs,
or confined in a dark, damp dungeon during the rest of the
week by other paid state officials. Why should I have believed
that this one state employee — the chaplain — should be on
the level any more than the others?

"To me a man with religion was a 'bug,' a 'nut,' or a 'molly-
coddle.'[1] I could stand for anything but that! But if I could
get what I wanted at this Mission I'd be a fool not to go.

"I stood outside looking at the joint and laughing to myself.
A bunch of suckers, I called them. They were Mission Stiffs,
I thought. Somebody was putting up the dough — some
cracked old nut — and those fellows down here were getting
away with it good and soft. I'd put one over on them.

"I went upstairs along with other men. It was very clean,
much cleaner than anything I'd seen in a long time. At the

[1] A pampered and overprotected person.

top of the stairs was a large room with a lot of poor fellows sitting around. A young lad came out of an office and said:

"'Good morning, what can I do for you?' I told him, and he pointed to a chair which he told me to take and he'd talk with me in a few minutes. Things were going all right I thought. I hadn't met as easy a bunch to work in a long time. It was like taking candy from a child. The warmth of the coal stove felt good too. It was a cinch!

"But the young fellow who was coming right back didn't come and I began to get leery and then I got sore! I was about to start something to show them I was wise when I felt a hand on my shoulder.

"They'd pulled a trick on me! I was pinched. I knew all the time these fellows with religion were crooked! I wanted to make a break and beat it when I heard a voice behind me, a soft, kindly voice:

"'Do you want a job?'

"I looked up and there stood a little old fellow with ruddy cheeks, dressed in a neat business suit, and I knew he must be one of those in authority.

"I looked about the room again. There were certainly twenty other men there doing as I was doing — waiting. Why had I been asked that question ahead of all the others? What was this fellow trying to hand me — something 'queer'? I didn't owe him anything — why should he want to do anything for me? He'd never seen me before and after I'd gotten what I came for he'd never see me again. I could have promised him that. What did he think I was? I looked at him again and he smiled as he repeated the question.

"'Do you want a day's work?'

"Before I realized what I was doing I'd said 'Yes.' It slipped out before I knew it. I didn't even say 'Sir' or 'Thank you.' Work! What did I want with work? How much honest work had I ever done? And then an idea flashed across my mind. I'd look the ground over; maybe I'd find a chance to get next

ch. ends next p.

to something. Maybe this job might help me to the coin I was after.

"They asked me my name and a few other questions and entered the information in a book of register. A card was given me introducing me to the firm to whom I was being sent, together with five cents for carfare.

"I was on my way to work! I went downstairs in a stupor. I remember how I laughed at myself for having been in a Mission and how I had fooled them. I've seen lots of other men since who thought they'd fooled the Mission when in reality they were the ones who were fooled, only they didn't know it at the time anymore than I did.

17.
Hard Manual Labour —
A New Sensation

"The address on the card read Seventh Avenue near Seventeenth Street. They had wanted help of a temporary sort, to carry lumber, and so they had telephoned the Free Labor Bureau of the Bowery Mission. And because I was a big-framed and strong-looking man, Charley Thompson (I learned his name on my way downstairs) had asked me if I wanted work.

"Here I was at the place and here was the lumber — a big pile of it. It was noontime and it certainly didn't look like the picking was going to be good for only laboring men were to be seen. Surely carrying that lumber all day was going to be no picnic. I was looking for something soft. All this makes it very difficult for me to understand why I took off my coat and with rolled-up sleeves went to work. It proved even harder than I thought it would but I kept on and was glad when the whistle blew at quitting time. The nickel for carfare I'd saved, for I knew it would buy me two early morning drinks and get me a place of shelter. That morning before I'd left the Mission I'd promised Charley Thompson that I'd come in to the service that night. I kept thinking about it all day. I'd made that promise like I'd made hundreds of similar ones to my wife — with not the slightest idea of ever making good. Every promise I'd ever made her I'd forgotten at once. But I kept thinking all day of my promise to that Mission Stiff!

"You know I was about as wise as they came, or I thought I was. Nobody could ever teach me anything. I had to be shown and that about a dozen times. I was 'from Missouri'[1] if ever a man was. I was suspicious of everything and everybody. A thing I couldn't understand was 'phoney' and a good thing to keep away from. I loathed everything churchy and all connected therewith were crooked. I tell you all this in repetition because you meet so many 'cons.' I wish every convict in the country could know my story. I believe it would make their 'comeback path' look brighter and easier to travel.

"When I quit work at 5:15 I was almost done up. My back ached and my arms ached. Ached like they'd never ached before. I was hungry as a bear. I could hardly wait to reach a meal. Seventy-five cents they had paid me and they told me that I could have another day's work if I wanted it.[2] Yes, I wanted it, and told them I'd show up. Work started at seven-thirty. I laughed at myself when I thought of it. Me at work at 7:30 carrying lumber.

"A heavy meal for fifteen cents made me feel a lot better. When before had I gone practically a whole day without a drink? It seemed like a year when I thought of it. My throat was cracking open for one. The price was in my pocket. It was there before my dinner and yet I'd gone by three saloons before I reached the restaurant. How do you account for it? I hadn't done a thing like that in years.

"On my way from dinner to the Bowery were at least fifty saloons. I entered only one and ordered and drank only two slugs — whiskeys. Mind you, I wasn't trying to quit the stuff, yet the fact remains that I only had two drinks. The

---

[1] Skeptical; unwilling to accept something without proof.

[2] Adjusted for inflation, that 75¢ would be approximately $25 in 2023.

previous night I'd 'a' stayed till the eighty cents was gone. Then, however, I spent just ten cents.

"Tell me, if you can, what took me to the service at the Mission that night? What made me keep my promise to Charley Thompson? I'd made my wife a thousand promises which were no sooner made than forgotten. Why did I keep my first promise to a stranger? At any rate, when the doors opened at seven, there I was, well up in the line. It was just the time when usually I was getting 'tanked up' down the street. I thought of that but decided to stay and see what kind of a show they ran. And it was some show, believe me! I don't remember ever being so interested and amused in my life. But I simply couldn't understand it. I thought the men were plum crazy as one after another they stood up and gave their testimony. One had been a thief, he said, and later a down-and-out, but had lost all of it since he'd given his heart to God. I thought someone had tipped him off about me and he was taking a chance on ringing me in as one of that bunch of old women! I was sure every man who spoke was paid for doing it. Surely no man in his right senses would get up and do it for nothing. They all, every one of them, talked about the same thing — Brotherly Love! Brotherly Love be hanged! How far would that stuff take me? What did I want with love? Love was meant for women — not men. Whiskey was good enough for me!

"At any rate I stuck the meeting out although I was disgusted long before it was over. Along with all the rest, some three hundred, I filed downstairs where we all got a hand-out — coffee and a big fresh roll. Again and again I asked myself what it all meant. It cost money — 300 rolls and 300 cups of coffee, 365 times a year. I spoke to a lad near me about it, and he said that from Thanksgiving to Easter, at one o'clock in the morning, the Mission ran a bread line where they fed upward of a thousand men. That cost a lot more! And then I remembered the Labor Bureau away upstairs. That cost more money! They didn't charge me a cent for the job

ch. ends next p.

they got for me. You know I didn't know anything about the Settlement in the Bronx or the Mother Bird Memorial Farm up in the Croton Lake watershed.

"As I went up out of the breakfast room to the street I decided I'd come in again the next night and see the show all over again. I told Thompson I would. They certainly were a soft-shelled bunch. I ought to be able to make it worth my while.

"Sleep came quickly when I got to bed. The day's work had exhausted me. I went straight to my 'pad' without a drink. I felt no wish for a drink or I would have had one, you may be sure of that. It was probably due to the fact that I'd been drinking very heavily the previous few days and after a hard drink a fellow's system sometimes rebels at booze. But if that's what kept me going that day and night with only two drinks it was the first time it had ever happened.

"I don't say what did it. I'm simply telling you facts.

"The following day, my second at the lumber pile, was twice as long as the first, twice as hard, and twice as profitable — profitable to the tune of $1.50.[3] And most of the previous day's pay remained in my pocket. Not a drink all day! Not one desire to steal! Another new sensation, that I thought about a lot and couldn't understand. All day I asked myself if I'd go to the Mission that night. Although I'd promised Thompson I would, about quitting time I decided not to. Another fifteen-cent meal and a good stiff hooker of whiskey and I felt good. I wanted it and I bought it. I wanted another and I bought that too. If I'd wanted more, like I had for years, I'd 'a' bought them too. But I didn't. Two whole days and not a drink — two nights and two drinks each. I was getting too good. I remember it made me feel like an old woman. I laughed at myself.

"But it made me think. And the more I thought the more puzzled I became. As I walked downtown I lost myself completely, so wrapped up was I in my own thoughts. After a

[3] Adjusted for inflation, that $1.50 would be approximately $50 in 2023.

while I woke up. I had stopped in my tracks and was directly in front of the wide-open doors of the Bowery Mission, the place where I didn't want to go. Curiosity got the better of me again. I'd go in and see the show. It was the middle of October, chilly, and I had no coat. Inside the Mission it was warm and there would be hot coffee and rolls. In I went!

"But I was wise and by the time the service was over I'd doped the whole thing out. Those men were bluffers. There was no other answer. Certainly no sane man would get up in a crowded public place and tell the bunch how many jobs he'd pulled off and how religion had saved him. That wasn't in the cards — they were fakers! I knew human nature and I knew that kind of stuff didn't go along with it. All this was side-show stuff. And I knew it paid well too. Oh! I knew it all in those days.

"There was another day's work for me at the lumber pile. I was tired. I needed the next day's pay, and if I wasn't on the job early and able to work with the rest of the crew I'd lose out. So another night I went to bed sober, this time without even one drink.

"Charley Thompson had told me to be sure and be on hand the next night for the Superintendent of the Mission, Dr. Hallimond, would be there and he wanted me to meet him. I said I would come and this time I meant it good and proper. If there was any easy money to be had out of the joint the man to get it from was the Boss. I'd make Dr. Hallimond fall for me all right.

18.

I Join the Brotherhood and Meet Dr. Hallimond

"I was dead set on meeting that Superintendent and I figured the best and easiest way to do it was to take a card and join the Brotherhood. After a fellow does that he meets the whole bunch and gets a chance to mix it up with them a bit. And so I decided to take a card that night.

"At the end of the meeting a couple of fellows came down the aisle, just like we do now, handing out the blank membership cards to all who would take one. I was wondering how many of the down-and-outs in the nearby seats would see me and laugh at me. I lost my nerve completely when the man reached me, and made no effort to get a card. But he stopped squarely at my side, stuck a card in my hands and said:

"'Take it anyway! It can't do you any harm.' I grabbed it eagerly. Here at last was a direct way to reach a man who had money to hand out to the likes of me and I was the boy to get it. But I got fooled that night good and proper! Like now, they made you hold the card overnight, ponder over it, and turn it in the second night. That meant I'd have to come in again. All right, the game was worth it.

"I was wise enough to know that it wouldn't do to have a 'stew' on or a 'hangover' on when I met Dr. Hallimond, and as I was tired out I again went straight to bed, the third consecutive night, dead sober. I had almost three dollars in my pocket too.

"For a long time I lay awake — thinking, and if you guessed till doomsday you wouldn't hit on what I was thinking about — that third night at the Mission. There had been a man on the platform who told us all what a raw run for her money he'd given his wife! He told us how he had mistreated her, and dishonored her. But say, he was a piker[1] alongside of me and the deal I'd given my wife. I couldn't help comparing the two of us as he spoke. And then he told us that it all had changed since he had come to the Mission! He told us that *Love* had done it. He told us how faithful his wife had been to him all the time he had been unfaithful to her. He talked like that for half an hour.

"For a long time I lay awake, as I say, thinking of that man and his story. I knew his wife couldn't have been treated worse than mine had been or for a longer time, and I knew too that she hadn't or couldn't have been more loyal than Jane had been.

"Suddenly something happened in my head. Then and there, in that dirty, filthy bed on the Bowery, I felt for the first time a feeling of remorse and shame. That's the truth. It was the first time in my life that I'd ever regretted anything I'd ever done.

"That man and his wife and his story kept ringing in my ears and flashing before my eyes! At last the crust of sin or rust or mildew, or whatever it was in which my conscience had been buried for years and years, was pricked. A tiny, tiny bit of light got in. *And I cried.*

"Sleep of a fitful sort at last overtook me but not before I'd realized that perhaps during all those years of her faithfulness I had unconsciously allowed to grow up within me something

---

[1] In this context: a mean or contemptible person.

ch. ends next p.

akin to love for that brave little woman. And now that something was trying to dig its way out, to find expression. And then, just as sleep was carrying me off, I made up my mind by all that was good and holy to do better by her and to start next day.

19.
Out of Work

"I finished that pile of lumber the following day — there was to be no more work at the factory. Why didn't it last and last and last forever? Why did that break come just then? Why was I put to the test so soon? Why couldn't it have come later when I was more nearly on my feet?

"Not a drink all day nor one at supper! I took a seat at the Mission, as far up front as I could get, and I held my card, already signed, in my hand.

"A fellow sitting beside me told me to turn it in because it was good for a bed that night. I nodded to him to let him know I was wise, but I didn't speak. I was thinking of Jane and the great wrong I had done her. The words of the man who had spoken of his wife the night before kept ringing through my head.

"The meeting was over. Charley Balevre[1] stepped up and greeted me kindly. Shook hands with me just like he meant it. As we walked upstairs to the Brotherhood Room he talked to me in a kindly, interested way about my work,

[1] Charles Balevre (1851–1928) was a jewelry merchant before becoming a leader of the Bowery Mission, and its organist for 20 years until his death.

and all the time he had hold of my arm. It was a little thing to do but it made a deep impression on me and so long as I live I'll never forget it. You see, even though I didn't know it, something was going on within me, something good was going on. The tiny little bit of light of the night before was holding its own — was still aglow.

"The room upstairs held a couple of dozen fellows seated here and there in a free and easy manner. Their ease was at once apparent to me. They were listening to a big, broad-shouldered, hearty-faced Englishman. It was Dr. Hallimond, the man I wanted to meet and beat. He had the kindliest and most sympathetic look I'd ever seen. At once I felt here was a man who was different! He came right over to me (I was a newcomer) and shook my hand in a hearty, genuine way that made my blood tingle. He said he was glad to see me. And he was! He's always glad to meet anyone in need. He's been glad for thirty-five years, doing that same thing all the time!

"Then Charley Balevre gave me my card of membership in the Brotherhood and he gave me also a pocket edition of the New Testament. It was with a sneaky, low-down feeling that I put it in my pocket. I didn't open it for fear I'd expose my ignorance of it and my contempt for it. Pretty soon we had a quiet off-to-one-side chat. Dr. Hallimond asked me a great many questions about myself and what I was doing and had been doing. He didn't ask me one embarrassing question. He branched off when he found he was on that track. He didn't scold me or lecture me, despite the fact that I told him some pretty straight stuff.

"All the time he was talking to me I kept thinking of my purpose in meeting him, and the more I thought of it the more I thought what a good fellow he was! Try as I would though, I couldn't understand him or why he treated me as he did, and no doubt all the others who came to him. As he rose to indicate to me that he had other things to do he put his hand on my shoulder and asked me if there was anything he could do for *me*.

"Here then was what I was looking for — an opportunity to get next — to do him — to put one over on him. The chance had come without the least effort on my part. He had broached the subject of his own accord. And on the tip of my tongue was a story waiting for him. The same kind of a story that had made many, many people come across whenever I'd sprung it. It was to be an easy victory.

"But the story remained on the tip of my tongue. It's there now! It's never been told! It's dead there! It died that night as I looked him in the face and replied that there was nothing I wanted of him.

"For the life of me I couldn't hand him the stuff — he was too kind — too good a fellow. I recognized it as kindness. It all dawned on me in a heap at that moment. For the first time in my life I felt I'd met up with an honest man — a man who was exactly what he professed to be.

"I went to bed that night without a drink, nor did I have the least desire for it. Not a drink all day, not one at night. I awoke early in the morning feeling strong and well and eager for work — for honest work of which there was none I could go to. Eager for work — me — the man I had been. That sounds strange I guess, but it's the truth. The factory was closed to me. The pile of lumber had gone. I'd carried it away. I'd been working four days and hadn't been drunk. In my pocket were a few hard and honestly earned dollars. In my heart was the first good thought that had ever been there. My wife's face with those drawn, pinched lines of hardship and sorrow appeared and reappeared to me all morning as I searched unsuccessfully up and down, here and there, for work. My new found hope and courage held all day but it was a fight. I didn't eat all day. With no work in sight there wasn't enough coin to spare for food. I was dreadfully tired from walking and my strength hadn't been helped any by

ch. ends next p.

fasting. The seats in the Mission, hard as they were, rested me, and the service, to a certain extent, had given me new courage. The only food I ate in those twenty-four hours was the Mission roll and cup of coffee at ten that night.

20.

In Which I Fall

"The next day and the next and the next brought me no work. Everywhere I went I was turned down cold. I didn't know how to apply for a job. Allowing for bed money and one meal a day my funds were good only for two days more.

"I kept out of my old haunts. I knew the necessity of that. Consequently I was very much surprised on meeting one of my former pals way off his usual beat — up above Cooper Square![1] He hailed me and put me wise to a 'busting' job. The employees of the American Locomotive Works at Schenectady, New York, were out on strike and the Pinkertons had the work.[2] I grabbed the tip eagerly and went after the job. I knew it would be an inside one and there would be no booze. In a 'busting' job like that they take the scab help, put them in the plant, and lock the doors. That's done to keep the scabs inside all the time and the strikers outside all the

---

[1] Cooper Square is a junction of streets in Lower Manhattan located at the confluence of the neighborhoods of Bowery to the south, NoHo to the west and southwest, Greenwich Village to the west and northwest, the East Village to the north and east, and the Lower East Side to the southeast.

[2] On October 26, 1911, *The New York Times* reported that 1,000 boilermakers walked off the job in Schenectady after the American Locomotive Works ordered them to work on engines for the New York Central lines whose boilermakers were already out on strike.

time. We slept on cots the firm provided. I got the job easily and the pay was four dollars a day — a fortune.[3] There was nothing to spend for board or lodging. I saw visions of a little home. I'd get a little place somewhere in a neighborhood where I was unknown. I'd take Jane there: we'd begin all over again and I'd be a good, kind husband to her. I believe I was happy on that job.

"It was then that I first took from my pocket the New Testament I carried. I read it, portions of it carefully, but I couldn't understand it, couldn't even make heads or tails out of it. It failed to make the slightest impression on me and yet I read and read again certain portions. If it hadn't been for my size and apparent strength the bunch would have had a lot of fun over it and over me, for they were a hard lot. They didn't like the way my sails were cut, so they kept quiet. One fellow, though, with whom I became quite friendly, told me he always thought he'd seen everything there was to see until he saw my Bible on a 'busting' job. It was a new one to him and I admitted it was to me as well.

"At the end of my first week I went to the boss and drew fifteen dollars against my pay. If you guessed for a week you'd fail on hitting on my object. I sent it to Jane! And as that money order left Schenectady for Brooklyn I experienced the most glorious sensation of my whole rotten life. I'd never felt so good before. Unconsciously I pushed out my chest, lifted up my head and looked my fellows in the eyes. Pride filled my heart and tears filled my eyes as I thought how proud and happy it would make Jane.

"That tiny little bit of light was still aglow within me. It had succeeded in breaking out. It had manifested itself to the world.

"The job lasted four weeks, and at the end of that time I received my money less the fifteen. It was a good sized roll for me and I felt rich. Some years before it wouldn't have been a consequence. However I bid the plant goodbye

---

[3] Adjusted for inflation, $4 in 1911 is equal to approximately $125 in 2023.

reluctantly and, together with about a dozen more of the 'busters,' began the trip down the Hudson by boat on the Night Line. No sooner were we aboard than the gang began to loosen up. Every one of us had plenty of money and the boat carried plenty to drink of every description. I knew trouble was brewing and I decided to quit the gang. I remember I thought I'd walk uptown. Then I woke up. I was on a boat and couldn't get away. I'd have to stay right there and fight it out on the spot. I went out on deck and walked away, firm in my determination to let the stuff alone, come what might. Around and around the deck I went. Each time I passed the entrance to the bar. Each time I passed it I felt stronger and better able to hold tight to my resolution. Each time I passed it I could look in at the door and see my friends crowded in front of the bar. At last I was beating rum. But all the same the fight was a bitter one. Several times I was on the verge of going in to have 'just one.' For two hours the game went on like that and then just as I passed the bar entrance out lurched one of the gang drunk as a lord and smelling like a distillery. He flopped right into my arms and invited me to come in and ''ave a smile.' That invitation in itself didn't faze me a particle, but the smell of the fellow's breath was too much. It was like a red flag in front of a bull. My blood turned cold and then hot. My system was on fire. I could have won that fight, I'm sure, if it hadn't been for the smell of the booze.

"I joined the gang and got beastly drunk. The stuff made me crazy and I didn't draw a sober breath until all of my 'roll' had been 'blowed' — about two weeks later. And before I had time to get thoroughly sober there was a strike in the Street Cleaning Department.[4] Wadell and Mahon had the job and I got a slice of it. Another long booze ended only when the coin ended.

---

[4] In protest over staffing and work conditions, over 2,000 New York street cleaners and garbage workers went on strike on November 8, 1911, with the strike lasting to varying degrees until December 11, 1911.

ch. ends p. 80

"It's a curious thing that from my last day at the lumber pile, which you will remember was a month or more earlier, I hadn't once been tempted to do any stealing, and not having been tempted I didn't steal. I can't account for it, but it's a fact. However, the desire came back strong after that big drunk following the Street Cleaning strike. When the time came that I had sobered up, a feeling of utter hopelessness came over me and I gave up the fight. I figured I could never get back with my wife. For the first time in my life I admitted to myself that I was a failure. My feeling of shame and remorse and sorrow was so bitter I gave up the fight — I quit 'cold.' I'd get a new 'roll' — I'd find a sucker and then I'd beat it for good and all.

"I was in the back room of a saloon when I reached this decision. I planned a western trip. Things were easier out there. Just then a strange thing happened. Like the day they'd taken me, handcuffed to Sing Sing, the big events in my life passed in review before my eyes. One by one I saw them. One by one they failed to move me — until last — like the first time — came the picture of my wife. This time, though, I first saw her as she had been when I married her, young, full of health and happy, and then I saw her as she looked the last time I'd seen her. Instantly my blood became afire — it boiled in anger and resentment against myself. I was all on edge and there in that back room I cursed myself over and over again.

"And then I quieted down. A new picture was before my eyes. I couldn't believe it, but there it was flashing ever brighter before me. It showed me standing in a room with a lot of men — men like myself — failures. A big man with a kindly face had his hand on my shoulder and was asking me if he could do anything for me!

"With a start that shook me to the very foundation I realized that I needed that man right then. I knew it! At once I left the gin mill and went uptown. Entering the Bowery Mission, I asked for Dr. Hallimond.

"He was confined to his home — slightly ill.

"I felt all in — heartbroken — ready to give up again. I wished I might die. As I was about to go downstairs and out on the street Charley Balevre spied me and remembered me, not as John Goode, but as a man who had some time earlier taken a card, and then had dropped out of sight. He came right over to me with out-stretched hand. He urged me to stay for the service and to come in regularly. He told me to come every day to the Labor Bureau and he would try and fix me up with enough work to keep me going until something permanent came along.

"God is good! He spoke to me that night if ever he spoke to anyone. I see it clearly as I look back on it now. My disgust with myself and my regret at failing to see Dr. Hallimond were sufficient to have driven me to anything. Charley Balevre saved the day: he said just what I needed to hear and he did it just as Dr. Hallimond would have done it.

"I went downstairs meekly and broken in spirit. I sang the hymns as I'd never sung them before and received great comfort and easement of mind from the service! They gave me a bed ticket and I was glad to take it for I wanted to be alone where I could think!

"Each day I went to the Labor Bureau and each day met the same kind treatment. This business of being kind to others began to soak in and the deeper it went the more ashamed of myself I became. You see I didn't associate my emotions with any phase of religion; if I had I'd probably 'a' quit — all I had in mind was Jane and a square deal for her. What these men did for me touched me deeply, but I couldn't figure it out. Here they were, total strangers to me, falling over one another to do me kindnesses. What had ever I done to deserve it? How had I treated those with whom I'd been thrown in contact? Finally I got to the point where I admitted to myself that there must be something real and tangible back of it all. When I arrived at that point I'd taken my second big step forward — out of darkness — into light.

ch. ends next p.

I realized then that this constant kindness to everyone stood for something definite. The men on the platform all said it stood for God!

"My third big stride ahead came next. If that was what God stood for — kindness — then I wanted God and I'd get God. From that moment on I was as serious as I could be, about that God business. I didn't understand it but I wanted to, and so I tried to do as they all did and I tried to pray. I was imitating instead of believing, so there was nothing doing.

21.
In Which I Suffer
as Never Before

"The next day an impulse overtook me which I tried hard to shake off. I wanted to go and see Jane. And yet I didn't want to go. I thought I ought to wait a little until I was surer of myself. But the idea wouldn't down and over I went.

"She was living then at her brother's home in Brooklyn. He had little use for me — justly — and I had as little use for him — just as justly. I found Jane with strength and courage gone. Her sister had just passed beyond into 'the other room' after a long and trying illness, during all of which time Jane in her already enfeebled condition had nursed her tenderly day and night. Poor little woman, she was indeed in a sorry plight. I never wanted to do anything so badly as I wanted to tell her about the Bowery Mission and what it was doing for me. Yes! and about what it *had* done for me. But I didn't. I thought it best to wait. I'd disappointed her so bitterly so many times that I preferred to wait and not run any chances of doing it again. But, oh! how my heart ached for her as I sat by her bedside! How I longed to do for her! I stood it as long as I could and, taking her in my arms, embraced her as

I should have done seventeen years before but had failed to do. And then I left her.

"As I passed out of the house into the street a great surging impulse stirred me: moved me like I'd never been moved before. I stood still in my tracks, closed my eyes, and offered up to Heaven this silent prayer:

"'Oh! God, if you're what they say you are over there in the Mission, give me the help I need — make me a good husband to my wife!'

"It was the first prayer I'd ever said. It was offered with all my heart and it brought me instant relief. I felt soothed and comforted and I walked with a lighter step and a braver heart. In that prayer I asked for all I thought I needed. But I needed lots else to make me a man.

"Without having had a mouthful of food all day I went to the Mission that evening. I'd walked to and from Brooklyn besides tramping around looking for work. I was exhausted. The music cheered me and I listened attentively to the men who testified to what good the Mission did them and to all God had done for them and was doing each day they continued to serve Him. I didn't laugh once that night! I tried as hard as I could to make it all seem real to me like it did to the speakers. And when they asked for requests for prayer I stood up and asked them to pray for me!

"Surely, surely I was making headway, and as soon as I sat down I realized it. I didn't feel ashamed — simply strange. And I left the service greatly strengthened physically by the coffee and rolls.

"Then began the period of most intense mental and physical suffering I ever went through. I'd had a hard life and had suffered all sorts of hardships but they were child's play alongside of my experiences until the following May — a period of about six months.

"I'd been one of twenty-five selected by Charley Balevre to form a Bible Class to meet with Dr. Hallimond on Wednesday nights for an hour prior to the big service in the Mission.

I was very proud of the chance, although it didn't mean very much to me, but I made up my mind to fight my battle to a finish.

"It was January and a bitter cold one at that. I don't think I possessed as much as seven pounds of clothing including my shoes. Both of them were nearly gone and I had no overcoat. I had neither work nor money. I went over the whole situation carefully and made up my mind that unless it was absolutely necessary I'd accept no favors from anyone at the Mission except, of course, work. And I was the same man who only a little while before had gone there to do them up! Such is the power of the religion of Jesus Christ — that's what they were taming me with.

"For days and days from ten till four I sat in the Labor Bureau sharing with my comrades the scanty calls for work that came in over the phone and by mail. I grabbed a ten-cent errand like I used to grab a thousand dollar roll. I tackled everything they offered me. There were days and days during which I didn't get a mouthful to eat except the roll and coffee at the Mission about ten o'clock, then one on the Bread Line at one o'clock. Night after night in almost zero weather I 'carried the banner' without an overcoat and with the poorest kind of broken shoes. Cold? Cold? Say, man, all you know about cold is how it's spelled! I've been so cold on some of those nights I didn't know where I was walking or even that I was walking. I got so cold I didn't know it was cold! And then how I suffered after sun-up on a warm grating over a bakery where I drank in the savory odor of freshly baked bread! You've walked a mile maybe in zero weather, on a good big breakfast and before a hearty meat dinner while you were warmly clad. Well I know what it means to walk in that weather all night for seven consecutive nights, scantily clad and not tasting one morsel of meat or fat in all that time. And what I got at the Mission taught me how to do that little stunt without complaining and without making a touch! Don't you call that a result? Do you think I did it for fun?

I did it because I wanted God and I couldn't get God unless I was on the level. Not once in that six months did I enter a saloon or touch a drop of beer or liquor or wine! Not once in that six months was I profane!

"One day while sitting in the Labor Bureau — half starved, helpless, almost hopeless and despairing of ever making good, I wondered whether it was worthwhile to go on. There were about eighty of us sitting about, and there wouldn't be eighty or forty or thirty jobs come in that day. There wasn't a chance in the world of my making so much as ten cents. Another night must I walk and walk and walk those icy, friendless streets till daylight. You couldn't stop or you'd die of exposure. I was on the verge of throwing up the sponge. God above knows how I was tempted, but I didn't yield. I sat still and grit my teeth. And then in the midst of my despair and discouragement in walked Charley Balevre. He must have read my face, for over he came and asked how things were going. Before I had time to answer he slipped a dollar bill into my hand and left me standing there. It was a gracious act and it came at a time when something unusual was needed to save the day. Never before or since has anything so strengthened me and put heart in me. A single, simple act! He had seen my desperate need. My soul cried to Heaven in thanks! I could sleep on a 'pad' again! I could have a piece of meat again! I could take off my clothes that night and have a warm bath. Do you wonder such thoughts made me feel good?

"On my way to a lodging house that night to rent a 'pad' I was told that the Holy Name Mission was to remain open all night because of the cold! In I went and also the four following nights — five nights of delightful, refreshing sleep, even though it came on a hard, wooden bench with my clothes on!

"Does God help a man 'comeback' while the man is on the level? Let's see! I was fighting hard. That January was the toughest of my life but I kept on right up to the verge of the breaking point. Then came that dollar bill! Then five nights of warm, restful sleep! And then the Mission gave me a job with board and a place to sleep in the Memorial House — a place they maintained where some of their converts lived! I was to tend door and the salary was one dollar a week. Every man in the house was living right and thinking right. I was thrown into intimate relation with these fellows and I got a lot of strength and courage to help me keep on struggling for a better manhood and for God!

"I attended the Mission services regularly and the Wednesday night Bible Class. My ultimate victory — although I fell down again miserably before I reached it — I lay to that six months' Bible study with Dr. Hallimond. When I got through the Bible meant something to me or rather a very small part of it did.

"We began our study at a happy Chapter. I doubt if any other would have 'got' me the way that one did. Perhaps the Doctor had more of my kind among the twenty-five. At any rate he chose well, for all of us, without exception, developed splendidly in our new life. We started and finished one chapter in those six months — the 13th Chapter of First Corinthians. Its undreamed of treasures were food to my starved soul. As the meaning of it — of love — dawned slowly on my mind I could see the beautiful way it had been applied to me and I realized at last that religion did have a 'kick' in it and that the brand I'd run up against, down there on the Bowery, was the real stuff. I understood then why they fed fellows and got them work as well as talked to them about God and his love. It was a different sort of brotherly love than I'd heard about in prisons and reform schools.

"Love — Brotherly Love — The love of God — His love for us — all these things became real to me then. I wanted to be on God's side — but only for Jane! I hadn't yet caught the true meaning. What I wanted God for was because of Jane.

"I thought she needed it in me. I didn't dream I needed it first. I didn't know then that I couldn't go safely — keep right until I got God for myself. But I learned that like I learned all I know by personal experience, the best teacher in the world.

ch. ends next p.

"From my dollar a week job in the Memorial House they transferred me to a job at a dollar and fifty cents a week in the industrial department at the Mission itself. I ate and slept there. My duties consisted of going out on call to collect old chairs that were to be re-caned and furniture that needed re-upholstering or repairing. This work was done in the Mission by men who were going through the same process I was going through. When the work was completed I delivered it and collected the money. They trusted me implicitly, of course, although they knew my past just as you do. I turned in every cent I collected and sometimes I carried a goodly amount of money. I did it all without an error and without even a single thought of being dishonest. You know what love and responsibility will do. Love is the most powerful force in the world and there is no power on earth can stop it once it gets into a fellow's skin. That's Mr. Osborne's belief and the results he's had at Auburn and Sing Sing are only natural and commonplace. He's awakening in the hearts of those men something they didn't know they possessed.

"As I called each week on Jane I could see plainly she was getting no better, in fact I saw she was failing. How my heart ached! And as I noticed this change for the worse in her she noticed the change for the better in me. Frequently she said to me, the tears streaming down her cheeks, 'John's a good man now!'

"While my salary had been a dollar a week I'd given her half of it, but now that I earned $1.50 I could spare her a dollar, which she got regularly. Those were proud and happy days for both of us! Each day that passed gave me greater confidence in my strength and my ability to beat the things that for years had beaten me.

"The month of May rolled round as I began to get impatient at the progress I was making. I wasn't earning enough. I wanted a home where I could take Jane. One dollar and a half wouldn't give it to me. And so I looked around for new employment. All my friends advised me to remain at or near the Mission, to stay where its influence could help me until I was stronger in my new life.

"But no, I must have more money. I must have a home for my failing wife. I feared she would die. I dreaded to think of that before I had in a small way made up to her for all those years of agony and heartache.

22.
In Which is Hell

"And so with the best and truest intentions in the world, with the positive belief that I was safe, I left the Mission. Many a man with position, ability, and education makes moves as disastrous as this one of mine. But in all such cases they are thought of merely as 'mistaken judgment.' In my case and in cases of others of my kind the verdict is 'willful backsliding.'

"I got a job in the Oceanic Hotel at Coney Island,[1] about the worst place in the whole world for me to go. I see it now and I saw it then, just after it was too late. About all I saw was drink. About all I heard was 'the ponies.' I was a porter and general utility man. The pay was a dollar and a half a day and my bed. The season was just starting. The sporting, drinking and gambling part of the public had been shut in the city all winter. They hailed the opening of the beaches and the tracks with delight. For a month I stood my ground solidly. I felt justified in the move I'd made. Jane was delighted at my willpower and strength. I didn't waver a bit — had not the slightest desire for drink or poolroom. Things went smoothly

---

[1] Coney Island House, later renamed Oceanic Hotel, was Coney Island's first hotel built in 1829 by the Gravesend and Coney Island Road and Bridge Company. It was the oldest building on Coney Island when it was destroyed by fire in 1930.

and well. If I had been aware of any temptation I'd 'a' beat it away. I feel sure of this as I look back at it now.

"But things couldn't go like that long. The environment was wrong and the good influence of the Mission and the men there was lacking. I was relying on my own strength and I hadn't enough to hold me.

"I fell; that's all. I didn't do it deliberately. The first thing I knew I'd been in Paddy Shea's poolroom — placed a bet — lost — and had a drink. The old life had me. It was all over. My system was on fire and I couldn't put it out. I went to the bottom — way, way down into the slime and filth of sin and shame. While it lasted I gloried in it. That must have been so else I'd never gone so far.

"You know what Jane suffered and what it cost her.

"I stole all she had saved of the money I'd sent her. I hocked her insurance papers and all else she had on which 'Uncle' would advance anything. It all went — every single pawnable thing! I'd go up there drunk, with a flask in my pocket and go to bed where I'd stay till the flask was empty.

"I'd been fired from my job at the Oceanic and had gotten one as a dishwasher at the English Kitchen on the Brighton Pike[2] at a dollar a day. Each night I drew fifty cents against my wage. That gave me a quarter for my bed and a quarter for booze.

"Day after day this went on and August came around. It was about the tenth of the month, I think, that I went up to see Jane. I was beastly drunk and wild from the effects of an unusually hard debauch. I staggered up the street and into the house. I went up to her room. There she lay!

"Her teeth were chattering. Her arms lay helpless at her sides. She didn't know me. She was trying to speak but couldn't. The neighbours were about. All was excitement. For a wonder I came partially to my senses. I telephoned

---

[2] In 1905, Brighton Beach Park opened its own amusements area named Brighton Pike, which offered a boardwalk, games, live entertainment, and a huge steel roller coaster.

ch. ends p. 92

and finally an ambulance came from Seney Hospital[3] and the brave little woman was taken away desperately ill from a stroke.

"As soon as she was gone the drunken rage returned and I broke loose more violently than ever before in my life. I ransacked the place, smashing things to bits. I found five dollars I'd missed before and stole that. As I was about to leave an insane impulse seized me and I lifted her trunk in my arms, hurled it through the door and down a flight of stairs.

"Off I went to Coney Island and began all over again. In a few days I sobered up sufficiently to remember Jane and went up to the Hospital to see her. She was somewhat better — enough so that she could speak. She saw me coming through the ward. Throwing her arms about my neck, she cried in agony and despair:

"'Oh, God, what will become of me now?'

"That scene and that cry and the look on her face struck terror to my heart. At once I was dead sober — as sober as I am now. I was a thinking man again. Man enough to have swallowed the poison I couldn't swallow before, if it hadn't been for the woman in front of me! And then my head swam. Perspiration stood out in beads on my forehead. My wife was going to die! No! No! It couldn't be! It mustn't be! There must be something I could do. And then it flashed across my mind — The Mission! There I could get help! I'd ask them. I'd write Dr. Hallimond.

"All the way back to Coney Island I thought of what I'd done. I cried to God for wisdom, for help — for the life of my dear wife. For the first time I felt that I had offended God — that God cared what I did. That feeling was very strong in me as I sat down and wrote to Dr. Hallimond.

"In the letter I made a full, frank statement. I told him

---

[3] Seney Hospital, also known as the Methodist Episcopal Hospital and later renamed Methodist Hospital, was located at the intersection of 7th Avenue and 6th Street in Brooklyn, New York. Today it is known as the New York-Presbyterian Brooklyn Methodist Hospital.

of the dastardly things I'd done. I asked him for help — for something — anything for my wife. 'For God's sake do for her — save her life.' For myself I asked nothing save forgiveness. I did ask that — I asked him to pray for me.

"For several days I awaited a reply from him. None came. What could have happened? Surely he was not throwing me over. No, I knew better. My anxiety was making me ill when a letter came postmarked Brooklyn. Who in Brooklyn would write me? Hastily I tore open the envelope and read the signature. The letter came from one of the members of the Wednesday Night Bible Class and his wife — Mr. and Mrs. Putnam. So long as God gives me the power to remember, this sentence from that letter will stay with me: 'If you don't come up to our house, and that right away, we'll have to come down there to you.'

"There indeed was *Friendship* and *Love* and *Kindness*. Dr. Hallimond, when my letter reached him, was laid up temporarily. At once he wrote to Mr. Putnam to get on the job and he hadn't lost a moment in doing so. Instinctively I knew that whatever there was to do for Jane had already been done. My relief was overpowering. I went all to pieces. I couldn't answer that letter; it broke me up when I tried to. Then another one came much like the first and I went up to their home — up Flatbush way somewhere.

"On bended knees we prayed long and earnestly.

"When I reached Coney Island a great load had been lifted from my mind. With Mrs. Putnam on the job I knew how Jane would fare. And until the day Jane passed away Mrs. Putnam was the good angel. Countless kindnesses and loving attentions she showered on my wife and became closer to her than any woman friend she ever had. Such is the power and love in the religion of Jesus Christ!

"With a set jaw I returned to my dishwashing and behaved myself. I finished the season at it and I finished without once side-stepping in any way. Jane recovered shortly, sufficiently

ch. ends next p.

to be moved to her brother's house and I again began sending her what money I could spare from my seven dollars a week.

"For some time before the end of the season I had longed for the Mission and its good friends — for the influence it exerted, but I wanted to get on my feet without their aid. At the close of the Mardi Gras I was glad to get away from the Island. The call of the Mission was strong upon me and I wanted more money. Jane was stronger and I wanted her to have her own home. That desire was stronger than it ever had been before.

23.
Together — At Last

"Back in New York never to leave it again! Back at the Mission! Back among my Christian friends! Back at the Labor Bureau! My strength and hope and courage returned to me many fold and thoroughly did I realize what it had cost — my leaving there that spring.

"Jobs didn't come in very fast and my money was almost gone when a wonderful thing happened. Wonderful because I was nearly broke and because I chanced to be around when it happened.

"The firm for whom I first went to work — piling lumber — needed an extra man, and as before telephoned the Labor Bureau.

"'Had the Mission a man to send over?'

"'Yes, the same man they sent before. Would he do?'

"'Yes, he had done well. Send him over right away.'

"And I went. They were busy and for about three weeks the work was steady. Nearly all my money went to Jane, of which she saved considerable. This time the work was a little more interesting and I became well liked by some of the men.

"Each day I prayed for strength to stand for God and for regular employment. And then came a day when the end of the work was in sight. I got talking with Bill Quarterly about my need of steady work because of a sick wife, and he asked me why I didn't make a bid for a steady job there. I told him I didn't know why.

"'If you don't I'll do it for you,' was his reply, and he did. Then and there I was added to the regular payroll.

"Without the slightest warning that it was at hand my greatest wish had come to pass. I couldn't believe it. It didn't seem real. I didn't deserve it. Ten dollars a week — five hundred and twenty dollars a year — with overtime amounting to possibly seventy-five dollars more.[1] And all with a reliable house doing a big, yearly business.

"A home at last!

"I didn't deserve it but Jane did and she would have it! And then — then — would I stick? With God's help I would. I knew that. At night I prayed to Him as I'd never prayed before that I might remain steadfast and true to Him. If I did that I'd remain steadfast and true to her. I had it right this time. I wanted to aid my wife through God.

"And God answered my prayer. He has kept me safe ever since. He left Jane with me for a little longer. He let me make up to her one hundred millionth part of what I owed her. He let me see her supremely happy. He let me help her make others happy. Yes, God is good!

"I told Dr. Hallimond about my good fortune — about answered prayer. I told him what I wanted to do, and the look that came into his kindly face told me to 'Go ahead.' And ahead I went. I took a dingy little room in the basement of a rooming house at 210 West 14th St., quite near my work.

"And then we had our honeymoon! My wife, myself, and God!

"There have been many honeymoons in this old world of ours, but there never was a happier one than that. The void that for seventeen years had filled her heart with anguish

---

[1] Adjusted for inflation, that's approximately $300 a week, $16,000 a year, and $2,400 in overtime in 2023 dollars.

and sorrow disappeared. God is good! Yes, indeed, He is! He brought us together but He spared each of us the knowledge that her illness was incurable, and that slowly but surely she must fail until it was time for her to go. He let our remaining nineteen months together be months of fuller joys than most men know. I can never thank Him enough for His goodness and mercy to me.

"The one room we called home I furnished with odds and ends from here and there and we began our housekeeping. At first Jane was well enough to walk the necessary three or four blocks to do the marketing. She was a careful buyer, for well had she learned the value of a dollar. In her hands my ten dollars went twice as far as I could have made them go. Our industrial insurance was always paid well in advance! The work at the factory went smoothly along and our happiness was complete.

"It was then immediately after our reunion that religion became most real to me. It became a living tangible thing, a force, a power that I could clothe myself with and make good use of each day I lived. My home, humble though it was, acted like a tonic on my tired, weary system. There was silver in my wife's hair and music in her laughter. I'd put the silver there and the music there. I couldn't take the silver away but I could prevent the musical laughter from ever going away. That was my job and an easier one no man ever had.

"'John, you're a good man now!'

"Over and over again she said that as she sat at her mending while I read.

"The Mission by now entranced me like the race tracks had done such a short while before. I became an assistant leader and then a leader.

"I stood on the platform and told my story to the crowd of men in front of me firm in the knowledge that somewhere in that crowd was a man I could touch like I'd been touched — firm in the belief that each time I told of the power of the religion of Jesus Christ I strengthened my own faith and foundation and strengthened the faith of each man who heard me.

"As time went on and I began to meet more right thinking people I became convinced that the reason men fall away from God is because they stop thinking. And so I planned what I had to say along lines calculated to make men see in themselves something I had formerly possessed. After a while I began to hear little things and see little things that made me feel that I too was spreading the story of love — of hope — that Jesus told — that I was helping others to something better. It made me wonderfully happy and gave me more courage and faith and strength. I went among the fellows in the meetings and learned to know them personally. And then after I'd go home Jane and I would talk over the men I'd met and wanted to help. Thus it was that God became so real to me. I saw Him at work and I worked with Him. I knew what He'd done for me. I could see it. My wife could see it. My friends could see it. It was real. My home and my new self were powerful testimonies to His realness. No argument could get away from those things. And I knew, too, that nowhere in the world could a man be found with a more unpromising outlook for success than I had had.

"The wonderfully beautiful part of life in that little basement room of ours were the Christian friends I'd made at the Mission. They all knew my story and they came regularly and gladly with delicacies and good cheer for Jane.

"There were rough times, too, when we'd close for a day or two at the factory. There were other times when calls on the cash were heavy for medicine. There were times when men we were interested in needed money more than we did. Many times there wasn't all we'd liked to have had, but always there was something else that all the money in the world wouldn't buy — the 'peace that passeth all understanding' and the knowledge that God is all-powerful.

"But like all happy times an end had to come. Jane grew more feeble. She could do less and less of the housework.

This I did at night. Finally she could do no more than crawl about from chair to chair and watch longingly between the gratings in our only window for my return.

"I left home early after getting breakfast and washing the dishes and didn't return till twelve-thirty for lunch. One day on coming home the shutters were closed and I was startled. And then inside, downstairs, our door was locked from within. In a second I'd walked right through it — frame and all.

"There on the floor in a great, wide pool of her own blood lay Jane with a two-inch hole in her skull from falling in a faint. And we sent her away to a hospital with a second stroke.

"More feeble than ever, she returned! Gracious and happy and contented she was! Not once had she ever scolded me or chided me or crossed me in any way. And here she was dying and I was helpless to save her. All I could do was to care for her in my primitive way. My friends would have sent her to a private room in a hospital, but she wouldn't leave her home or her John! They would have sent in a nurse, but she would allow no one to care for her but 'John.' Even after she was unable to recognize them they came and came and came — these friends of ours — these friends so full of brotherly love.

"On the advice of at least three doctors I kept her alive on whiskey for the last few months. My wife was dying under my very eyes. I'd had to give up the little home where we'd lived and loved. I was powerless to help her. But I bought her whiskey and I fed her whiskey for weeks and weeks and weeks and not a drop of it ever touched my lips. Oh, God is good! Think what He saved that woman from as she lay there dying! God is good!

"At last she required more care than I could give her — you know the rest — how we sent her to Bellevue[2] and how she died. You were there!"

[2] Bellevue Hospital, located at 462 First Avenue in the Kips Bay neighborhood of Manhattan, New York City, is the oldest public hospital in the United States.

ch. ends p. 100

*

John Goode's huge frame shook convulsively while unchecked tears rolled down his cheeks. They were tears of sadness and shame, of joy and victory all in one. The floodgates of an intense nature had broken open. Such tears are difficult to check even when there is a will, but there was no will now to check them. There are times when naught save tears will bring relief, and this was such a time.

Instinctively my mind went back to that clear, cold October day when Jane lay so sick in Bellevue Hospital!

Was it the guiding hand of Providence that had forced this man and his desperately sick wife into my mind as I worked at my desk that day? Was it the guiding hand of Providence that had kept me uneasy all day until at half-past four I could stand it no longer? I put on my hat and walked over to the factory where he worked and together we went around the corner to their dingy basement room where they had been so wondrously happy for over nineteen months. We went to that room which had been a retreat from storm and temptation for so many, many human derelicts — to that room which had shared its all with any who asked by day or by night, to that room which had seen so much of physical pain — to that room which was to be his home no longer!

Graciously and hospitably he prepared a frugal meal. The dishes we left unwashed. We hurried to the street.

Vividly I remember, remember as though it were but yesterday, how from a flower vender at Sixth Avenue and Fourteenth Street he purchased ten cents worth of perfumed sprayed roses for the frail, sick little wife lying in her bed of pain in that ward at Bellevue.

And again we had hurried on. Neither of us spoke.

We entered the ward. Her bed was empty and had been

freshly made up. My heart almost stopped. He did not seem to realize the significance of that empty bed.

A nurse tiptoed up and beckoned us to follow. Jane had failed rapidly late that afternoon and they had telegraphed for him to come at once. But the telegram had miscarried.

Beyond the shadow of a doubt it had been an act of Providence that had compelled me to act, as that telegram failed to reach him.

They had moved the almost worn out little frame to a private room. The bed lay close to a partly opened window.

Preceded by the nurse, we entered at precisely the moment that nature gave way and the poor, tired, worn out little heart ceased its beating forever.

Those flowers — he could not hand them to her now — he laid gently on her breast.

What a night that was! How brave he had been! How manly — how totally unlike the man he formerly had been — how much like the man so many of us ought to be.

We walked the streets, going nowhere, but always walking, walking, walking till long after daylight. It was bitter cold, but he felt it not. He was fighting — fighting the biggest battle of his life. Fighting to resist the old call — the call of drink, of excitement, of anything to deaden the pain at his heart.

And he won his fight!

His tears ceased and our eyes met. We read each other's thoughts. Why shouldn't we? Fate had served me as she had him. He had been to me under similar circumstances what I had been to him. Together each time we had passed through two never-to-be-forgotten events.

★

"You know how we took her little body to the Mission that the men there might see the lesson in her life — you know the memories that service awakened in the hearts of many

ch. ends next p.

men long since separated from their dear ones as I had been. God alone knows how much good that service did.

"You remember how we cleared the room out, destroyed what I didn't want and gave the rest away? It was all over then. And when the excitement had passed off and the old, old wanderlust again crept into my being I packed up my belongings, for I was afraid.

"With my bundle in my hand, and with the fear in my heart that I'd fall, I went back where my real, true self came from — I went back to live again at the Bowery Mission.

Epilogue

John Goode is by no means an imaginary person. The fore-
going story is not, as some might suppose, either romance
or fiction. The graphic recital of this man's uplifting from
the lowest depths of depravity to the pure, clean heights of
a thoroughly regenerated manhood, is not open even to the
charge of exaggeration. Speaking under the mighty stress of
an exaltation and rapture unknown and unknowable except
to those who have been delivered from the thrall of gross
materialism, and have become "new creatures in Christ
Jesus," extreme language, with an occasional trip across the
border into the purely imaginary, might almost have been
pardonable.

But nothing but hard, cold, and sometimes cruel fact has
fallen from this man's lips.

The temptation to the author, Mr. Scandlin, must also
have been a very great one. The friendship between these
two men has been one of the most pathetic things I have
ever known. Utterly dissimilar in disposition, training, and
temperament, the one a young businessman, the other a
hardened ex-convict, they were brought together in the
Bowery Mission, learned together at the feet of the Great

Teacher the same lesson of Love, and formed for each other an affection and respect never surpassed since the days of David and Jonathan.[1]

Notwithstanding this, Mr. Scandlin has conducted the recital of this touching story without permitting a hair's-breadth deviation from the line of absolute fact.

The story could very well be extended, and something said of John Goode's life of abundant usefulness during the last few years. He is one of our most active workers, the leader of our Wednesday night meetings, and the assistant leader of the Sunday evening meetings. He is never absent from his post. He puts an amazing amount of enthusiasm into everything he says and does, in connection with the meetings. When he speaks, he never remains on the platform, but walks down into the midst of the crowd, where he has his audience at close grips. His talks and testimonies are always delivered with tremendous force, and many a brand has he plucked from the burning.[2]

His activities, however, are not confined to the meetings. If there is any poor outcast, who has fallen so often that even the warm-hearted workers in our meetings have lost faith in him, it is John Goode that goes after him. If the news comes to the Mission that some man has fallen by the way, been overcome with temptation, and is in the backroom of some saloon, or has been taken to the Tombs prison, or the alcoholic ward of Bellevue Hospital, it is John Goode that always flies to the rescue. His own deliverance has been so wonderful, and his faith in God and man, therefore, so great that he despairs of no one. He is a man of great mental ability, he has a passionate love of reading works of philosophy, poetry, and artistic literature. He has two favorites amongst the preachers of New York City, whom he never fails to hear

---

[1] David and Jonathan were, according to the Bible's Book of Samuel, heroic figures of the Kingdom of Israel, who formed a covenant, taking a mutual oath.

[2] A reference to Amos 4:11 and Zechariah 3:2, meaning his testimonies connected with those meant to still make their marks in life. How many brands have you plucked from the burning?

when he has the chance, Dr. Jowett[3] and Dr. Hugh Black.[4] Readers of this little story, bearing in mind his early training, and his progress through the dark byways of vice and crime, may be surprised to know that the two principal features of his character are his love of the beautiful and his love of little children.

There, perhaps, never was such a service in the Bowery Mission as the Memorial Service to his wife. He insisted upon having her body brought and placed in the middle aisle of our auditorium, and as he stood there, his huge frame shaking with emotion, his hand resting lovingly upon the casket, he pleaded with the men, especially those separated from their wives and children, to accept the same wonderful salvation that had come to him. I have been many years in this work amongst the lowly of the Bowery, and have witnessed many pathetic scenes, but amongst the most impressive are those of that faithful wife in her humble home in her later days, rejoicing over the answer to her prayers, and the transformation of her husband. Over and over again, with a smile of ineffable beauty resting upon her poor, worn features, would she repeat the words, "John is such a good man."

We are praying that John Goode's life may be spared to us for many years to come, for a stouter, braver life has never breasted the waves in behalf of his fellowmen.

J. G. HALLIMOND,
Superintendent of the
Bowery Mission.

---

[3] John Henry Jowett (1864–1923) was an influential British Protestant preacher who wrote books on topics related to Christian living and served at the Presbyterian Church, Fifth Avenue, New York, from 1911 to 1918.

[4] Hugh Black D.D. (1868–1953) was a Scottish-American theologian and author who emigrated to the United States in 1906 to accept the position of chair of Practical Theology at Union Theological Seminary in New York City, then later became pastor of the First Congregational Church in Montclair, New Jersey.

John Goode Doing Good Work

DURING the last two months John Goode, whose remarkable life story was recently published in the Christian Herald, has related his experience to large and deeply interested audiences in many churches in different states. In several places he has spoken at more than one service, and, besides addressing church congregations, he has responded to invitations from missions, Sunday schools, brotherhoods and men's meetings. In a number of places the attendance in some of the churches was the largest ever known in these buildings. His Gospel tour includes the States of New York, New Jersey, Connecticut, Pennsylvania and Massachusetts. On every occasion he was most cordially received, and the audiences were sympathetic and responsive. At one of the meetings he spoke to an audience of 750 in the town hall, by special arrangement.

Evidences were not wanting at many of these gatherings, showing that the wonderful story of John Goode's transformation by divine grace fell like good Gospel seed upon hearts that were ready to receive it. Told in his own quiet, simple way, it is an experience that never fails to kindle an audience to sympathy, and many a man after the meeting has grasped the speaker's hand and thanked him for having brought a new light and nobler purpose into his life.

Mr. Goode relates this experience in connection with one of his services in a New Jersey city within twenty miles of New York:

"After the meeting one of the congregation told me that a young girl, who had attracted my attention by her lovely contralto voice, wanted to speak with me. When I went to her she told me she wanted my assistance in locating her father, who was living in a Bowery lodging-house. She gave me the name of a well-known house of the cheapest type, and said that perhaps the day or night clerk might know where her father could be found. Two or three days afterward I went to see the clerk and asked him if he knew a man by that name. He said he did, but he was not a lodger in the house, although he called there frequently. I left a message, asking him to call and see me at the noon-day prayer meeting in the Bowery Mission.

"Several days later he called. In my talk I told him how anxious his little girl was to help her father and to do everything she could to get him to try and be a good, strong man again. A meeting was arranged; on a certain night she was to come over and meet her father in the Mission, and they were to have a heart-to-heart talk together. It was a memorable night. After the meeting the choir and members and their pastor went down to the breakfast room, and sang to the men of the Bread Line while the poor wanderers were having their coffee and bread. It touched profoundly all who witnessed it, to see the little girl run over and kiss her father between the iron gratings that separated the aisle and breakfast-room, as the men came down to their meal. It made an impression upon the hearts of the Mission workers that will never be effaced—a tender, loving little girl leading her father back through the force of her faith and love.

"That father was at the Mission services the next week, well dressed and happy-looking, sitting on the platform, while his dear little daughter was singing for the men of the Bowery with a face that radiated God's own spirit of the Eastertide. To me it was an illustration of the sacred truth that 'love never faileth.' God's love, working through the heart of a child, had won the father back from sin and suffering—won both soul and body, for he is leading a Christian life today."

Pastors of churches within 100 miles of New York who desire to have John Goode speak to their congregations can address him in care of the Christian Herald. Dates will be arranged by mail.

"The Wicked John Goode"
By HORACE W. SCANDLIN

Introduction by THOMAS MOTT OSBORNE. Epilogue by REV. J. G. HALLIMOND

A book full of thrills — a book with a message. The runaway lad — the reform school — the state prison — the drunkard's reward — the whole gamut of life's tragedies right through to Christ and redemption. Life at its worst and best.

THE CHRISTIAN HERALD, Bible House, New York

James Goode
HONORARY HEATHEN

Appendices

To Mr. Scandlin, prisons are a hobby. Not a fad, but a subject for deep study, deep interest, deep feeling.

He has lived with crooks. Crooks have lived with him. He has helped them in jail. He has helped them out of jail. Many of his present-day friends, commonplace businessmen now, are ex-convicts and ex-crooks.

He knows what he's talking about when he's on the subject of prisons.

The "homey" atmosphere in this Sing Sing cell (seen at right) is the result of the efforts of a prison reformer, since discredited and put out of office by the politicians of New York state.

Does the lock-step lead naturally back to the prison gates, and do stripes spoil their wearers for citizens' garb? All medical cases in a hospital are not cured with the same medicine, nor is the same operation performed on all surgical cases. Then why treat all cases of crime in the same stereotyped way?

The Prison of Today
Does Not Cure Crime

The prison of tomorrow must be a better one than the prison of today.

America's whole social structure is in a stage of transition.

Thousands of illiterates await the unlocking of our ports of entry.

Thousands of foreign born population refuse or are unable to absorb what we call Americanism.

We turn loose each year from our penal institutions more than half a million criminals.

In the congested sections of our large cities we operate training schools for crooks with at least a million and a half juvenile pupils.

The divorce courts and the domestic relations courts see the making of hundreds of delinquents.

The prison of tomorrow must be a better one than the prison of today.

So soon as one begins to agitate a change in our prison system so soon is he charged with being either a sore head or a sentimentalist. Yet the fact remains that rarely have our prisons done more than confine criminals for the duration of their sentences. If that, and that alone, is what prisons are for, then ours have been eminently successful — far more so than our schools or colleges or our public utilities.

Years ago in the United States there were on our statue books more than a score of crimes for which the penalty was death. Consequently there were comparatively few men confined in prison — most of the offenders being confined three feet down under quick lime and sod.

Then the idea was introduced that a prison should be a place of correction. That law breakers should be confined for a given period of time. The fixing of the time limit was placed practically in the hands of one man — a judge. So it is today.

Thomas Mott Osborne, the greatest of all prison reformers, a man with ideas fifty years ahead of his time, has asked what physician there is who would say to his patient, "You have smallpox. You must go to a hospital. In exactly four and a half weeks you will be cured. You can be released at that time."

Yet we do precisely that with our criminals — by specifying their term of confinement we predict the exact time they will be fit for society again.

We do even worse. A reformed criminal, a man who was arrested the first time at fifteen years of age and who was sent away the last at forty-five said to me recently: "I learned more wrong inside than outside. On the outside I put into practice the theories I learned on the inside. The inside is the best training school I know."

A prison population represents all classes of society. There is the college graduate and the illiterate. There is the gentleman and the tough. There is the kind-hearted, sympathetic individual and the brute. The minister, the atheist, and the near idiot. The man physically sound and the man horribly diseased. Youth and old age. There they are herded together — all doing practically the same sort of way-down-the-scale manual labor — a sorry crowd, a sorrier sight, and the sorriest commentary on our twentieth century civilization to be found anywhere in the United States.

Were you to contract a prison population with an equal sized group of men selected from the same strata of society who never had served time you would be mightily shocked to find that the *chief difference* between the two groups lay in the fact that those in confinement had all been caught, tried, convicted, and sent away.

The most gentlemanly man I ever knew served four prison terms. The bravest man two terms. The kindliest man two terms. The worst brute I know has never been in prison. Nor has the cruelest man I know. One of the clearest thinking men in the country was a bandit of the worst order for years and years and died a pardoned and respected citizen of the state of New York.

One of the most serious faults of our prison system is that it is too closely mixed up with politics. Until the prisons are far removed from the machine boss they will fail to function efficiently.

Few men leave prison in as good mental or physical condition as when they were admitted. Their faith in themselves and in mankind is shaken. Their vision is clouded. The manhood in them has well nigh disappeared. The animal in them has been over-developed.

It is a simple enough matter for an ill-tempered or dyspeptic[1] judge to say "Ten years," or "Fifteen years." He gets used to it. But as prison conditions exist today the same judge would be far more charitable were he to say "For life."

We must not forget that the majority of the men we send away are some day coming back. They are then going to walk the same sidewalks we walk, use the same cars we use, the same hotels and restaurants. They are going to rub elbows with us and with our families. It is of vital concern to us the manner of man we turn loose from our state prisons. But who would guess it from our attitude?

---

[1] One who suffers from indigestion or irritability.

ch. ends next p.

Prisons cost money — very much money. The public pays the bills. The convicts usually have dependents whom they leave behind in the great outside. Thousands become wholly or partly dependent on charity. The cost is great. The public pays.

And in the meantime friend convict is leading a life worse for *him* in many ways than the life he led outside. He earns so little it may be called nothing without fear of contradiction. He works, the state will say. Yes, he works. Just as hard as we would work were we in his place. But does he work as hard as if he knew that his efforts were putting food in his loved ones' stomachs and clothes on their backs?

The ways of the world have gone ahead pretty fast in the last century — in spots.

We live in strenuous times.

What the next decade holds in store no one can tell.

There are cancers in the body politic.

They need surgical treatment.

The prison of tomorrow *must* be a better one than the prison of today.

Horace W. Scandlin
World Outlook
December 1919

Hopeless, helpless, useless!
The result of a system maintained at high cost to society; a system which, instead of preventing crime, teaches and encourages it.

———

When children who need only to be spanked are instead sent to reform school, the process of making criminals is begun. There they learn the foundation principles of crooked living.

Later, when they try putting these principles into practice, they almost inevitably land in prison for a more advanced course. That menace to society — the ex-convict — is the final result.

Prison Products

Since the oldest one among us can remember, the penal institutions of the United States have been turning back into society's midst those convicts who have paid the penalty of the law. The iron doors swing open, the man pulls his cap down over his eyes and the public swallows him up. And as promptly forgets him! As a matter of fact, the public forgot him the day sentence was passed.

To one who knows these men well it would be highly amusing were it not so sad and serious a business to see the fuss raised and to read the newspapers after "a desperate criminal" has escaped from prison. Cases have been known where dogs were put upon the scent, where men with guns went out upon the trail ready to kill if necessary the "escaped convict."

What sort of men are the convicts? Do they think? And cry? And laugh? And love? And hate? We do! Or do they arm themselves with knives and guns? Do they lie in wait to jump at the throat of Mr. Unsuspecting Public?

In what twenty years ago was "the tenderloin" in New York City there is an old cellar. It is like thousands of other New York cellars. But few cellars in all the world have harbored the crowd or listened to the conversations that this cellar has. It was Billy's cellar then and it's Billy's now. It always will be "Billy's Cellar" long after Billy is through and has taken up his work in the Great Beyond.

I counted myself more than fortunate the day I was granted the freedom of the place, and Billy, with one hand on my shoulder, turned to the gang and said, "Fellows, he's all right!" That was my introduction. It was simple and final. The fact that it had taken me five years to get it is another story.

Just a word here about Billy. He was a bad boy. He needed a spanking. Instead he was sent to a reform school at eight years of age. There he was turned loose among older boys who knew the crooked game from start to finish. Before Billy was released — or before the authorities had reformed him — he knew the crooked game too, but only in theory. As soon as he was free he put his reform-school-learned theories of how to go crooked into practice. He tried it time and again. Naturally he went clear to the bottom of the chute and on the way spent twenty-one years in prison. During all this time he didn't improve, of course. In everything he undertook he went the limit. Once, out of prison, he cut a policeman's intestines open with a long, sharp knife. Once, in prison, he cut another man almost to bits. But all that is a thing of the past — that side of Billy is dead — that was twenty years and more ago. For more than ten years he has worked for his present boss. I've known him to pawn his watch and best overcoat to help a needy friend. I've known him to work all night and turn his overtime in to help buy medicine and care for a sick child, and the kiddie didn't belong to him but to a stranger. Billy found a power that had a real live "kick" in it, and he's never once let go. *But the point is that he didn't find it in prison!*

Billy's cellar has always been a "hang out" for ex-convicts. Strange indeed are the characters that have hobnobbed there. Many and many a time I've sat in the circle of boxes, and

barrels, and broken chairs, and marveled at and almost cried
over some of the talk I've heard.

Do such men think? And cry? And laugh? And love? And
hate?

One stormy afternoon I dropped in on Billy, for I knew
the retreat would be well filled. "Red" Dugan was talking.
He is sixty years old. Exclusive of workhouse time, which
he refuses to dignify as time, "Red" has served forty years
behind locked doors. He is a useless, helpless product of a
worse than barbaric system. He is broken in health, a mis-
erable drunkard and an infamous liar. Yet as one of God's
creatures he receives one meal a day and a bed to sleep in
from the frequenters of Billy's cellar. "Red" began to steal
when he was six years old. He was doing "time" at eight.
Listen to him at sixty! He's talking about Sing Sing prison:

"Me an' Joe was 'doubled up' in eight gallery back in 1880.
Him an' me done six years 'doubled' in dose little stone slots.
Joe had more'n half his 'bit' in, an' me, I wuz goin' out in two
days. De t'ought o' goin' home made me nervous. I couldn't
lay on me bunk — couldn't eat nuttin'. I wus all in. Me an'
de gallery man wus figurin' out a swell deal I wus ter pull off
downtown as soon as I got me bearin's. He had a pull wit
de P. K. (principal keeper) an' fixed it fer me ter stay in me
cell Saturday. I wus goin' ter be 'sprung' Monday. I didn't
dare mix it up wit de boys in de yard or de shops — I was
too nervous. I'd a fought sure an' got de cooler besides losin'
me 'short time' (good behavior credits). Yer know I wuz just
finishin' a twelve-year 'bit' an' me hide wus itchin' fer ter
git out an' at it agin, so I daren't take no chances. I'm after
tellin' yer I couldn't be still; so wit me han's in me pockets
I walked up an' down me cell de whole day. T'ree steps east,
turn around, t'ree steps west, turn around; t'ree steps east,
turn around, t'ree steps west. De whole day I done dat wit me
han's in me pockets — t'inkin' o' de job I wus goin' ter pull.

"Joe tried ter make me eat, but it wus no use. I wus nothin'
but nerves, nerves, nerves. I had ter keep goin' and Joe, de

ch. ends p. 121

good skate, stood up all night at de door o' de cell so's I could walk. I wus a'scarcd ter leave me cell Sunday — me nerves wusn't holdin' good. I kept walkin' all dat day too, till about eight o'clock, when I sat down 'cold.' Joe wus a'scared ter touch me fer fear I'd come around an' begin me walkin' agin. He just t'rew me blanket over me, let down de upper bunk, climbed in an' hit de hay.

"Monday I wus worse dan before, but I pulled meself together, told Joe 'So long' an' beat it, wit de Chaplain tellin' me he was sure I'd be back again soon.

"He wus right, dat minister was, fer I was back in seven weeks wit a five-year 'package' hangin' round me neck fer 'prowlin'.'"

"Red" Dugan is but one of thousands. Forty years of that sort of confinement have rendered him immune. His kind needs love and kindness and responsibility. In or out of prison? In prison, most assuredly! But in any different prison from any he has seen.

A man I had never met before sat shivering in his soiled rags as close to the warm steam pipes as he could get. One look at the poor creature was enough. I turned my eyes away in horror. He was nearly through. His lungs were almost gone. He had broken one law only once. In a drunken rage at twenty-two he had killed a friend in a row over a girl. His former record had been good. Yet it made no difference. He was treated to the same punishment served a confirmed pickpocket. What an interesting result we would achieve were we to give all our hospital patients a dose of the same medicine? One is as reasonable as the other. At the start he wasn't a strong man. The dampness of the cell he lived in, the wretchedness of the food he ate (I have eaten with the men at Sing Sing), and the impurities of the air in which he performed his daily task, beat him down, down, down in health until tuberculosis held him in its grip. And then you and I — the public — let him go, helpless, hopeless, desperate.

We put him out, alone, to roam the streets, unemployable, living as best he could — until death mercifully claimed him. An eye for an eye! A tooth for a tooth! A life for a life! Surely a corrective system!

"Billy," said I, "did you ever try to go straight on leaving prison?"

"Never in me life till Mrs. Booth got her hands on me," he replied.

"You made good. How do you account for it?"

"God bless yer!" (Billy's eyes always get watery when he says that.) "It wusn't as hard as I t'ought it would be when I seen how she wus goin' about it. Yer see, I didn't know nuttin' dat wus right. She knowed dat, too, an' so she says ter me, 'William, yer do as I tell yer.' An' yer can bet I did!

"Did I git meself a job?

"God bless yer, no! I didn't know how. She got de job fer me. She told me what ter do an' what ter say, an' she told de General what engaged me de kind of a guy I wus.

"Say, dey couldn't 'a' been kinder ter me if I wus de General's own son!

"Yer see, dey knew right well how queer it wus fer me to be obeyin' anyone what didn't have a gun or a loaded stick or a dark cell ter dump me into if I put up a kick.

"I made some breaks, believe me, but, say, dey wus on de square wit' me, an' it wusn't long before me old hide begun ter thaw out an' I begun ter git wise ter what wus expected.

"God bless yer! Every time I put a good one over she wus as pleased as if she'd made a t'ousand dollars.

"Dat's all what done it — dat's just what kept me goin' all de time. All de time me fingers wus itchin' an' me tongue hangin' out fer a drink. Just bein' kind an' good ter me an' tellin' me der wus a God, an' a good One, too."

A bright, clean-cut, well-dressed, able-bodied, ruddy-faced youth of 24, whose mind, despite three prison terms, is as keen as a razor blade, and who is a very real friend of mine, was in the circle. Listen to him. Judge how dangerous

ch. ends next p.

and unbalanced a chap he is, and how frightened I must have been as I sat facing him.

"The next time you discuss this question of heredity and you are at a loss for a clinching argument, remember me. I know a street in Brooklyn, on one side of one block of which seven little boys grew up together. These seven were typical of the children of the neighborhood. Many years later, or December 1915, to be exact, one of those former little boys died — an ex-convict. Another lay in a hospital with a serious stab wound — he also was an ex-convict. The remaining five of that original seven, myself one of them, were all serving prison terms in the State of New York."

Said another lad of twenty-four:

"Heredity be hanged! I was a bad boy, with older companions and without restraint. I went the limit until I came in contact with a personality that reached me. I'm through with the old ways. I'm happier than ever before but as poor as a church mouse."

How terrifying it must be to associate with "a dangerous criminal" who talks like that. This particular chap took part in two jail deliveries.

"Pikey" B—— is a man about thirty-three, one who has served three terms in prison. I have never heard of a more glaring injustice being done an ex-convict than an experience he had just been through. Six months before he had come down from Sing Sing to begin all over again — straight. A friend secured him a job. At the start the salary was $10 a week. At the end of the second month the boss voluntarily raised the wage to $12 and gave Pikey to understand that with continued good work he might expect $80 a month at the end of the first year. Pikey's joy knew no bounds.

And then — and then someone who knew Pikey's past told his boss the story. Pikey swears it was a "flattie" (policeman), and it looks very much as though such were the case. The boss asked Pikey why he hadn't told of his prison record.

"Because yer didn't ask me," Pikey told the man.

"Well, here's your week's salary. Now get the hell out of here!"

I looked at Pikey and Pikey looked at me. His face was a puzzle.

"What did you say to him?" I asked.

"Nuttin'!"

"What did you do?" I was curious.

"I hit him a puck[1] in de eye an' beat it!"

In spite of me I couldn't but remember that the fellow had two eyes.

"Did you do anything else, Pikey?"

"Yes! I went out an' got beastly drunk, an' I didn't quit till I'd blowed me roll!" (Spent all his money.)

And while the debauch was on it has been Billy who took care of Mrs. Pikey.

Horace W. Scandlin
World Outlook
January 1920

---

[1] A sharp blow; punch.

What Kind of Citizens Do Our Prisons Turn Out?

Prison departments and prison officials have at their finger-tips quantities of records and statistics with which they build up a defense of their work.

It is all "like unto a house built upon the sand."[1]

Such figures are utterly worthless when compared with the men to whom they refer. I know 500, perhaps more, convicts and ex-convicts. Many of them I know very well. Some of these friendships have run over a period of many years. I know what these men think, and hope, and believe — those few who believe anything. I have eaten with them and lived with them. I am interested only in facts — theories are useless when dealing with strong-willed, red-blooded men. The public, too, wants facts.

And the facts are these: In a broad sense, the prisons of this country are no more than huge detention places, operated along lines of policy that degrade, humiliate, and crush. There is nothing about prison life that tends to lift

---

[1] A reference to The Parable of the Wise and the Foolish Builders, also known as the House on the Rock, a parable from Jesus' Sermon on the Mount in the Gospel of Matthew (7:24–27).

up, encourage, or fit a man to earn an honest living on the outside. All those things are securely fastened against the outside of the outside door.

The effect of our prison system is destructive — not constructive.

We have been turning loose from our State prisons thousands and thousands of men each year. What sort of men were they in the beginning? And what sort when they were turned loose?

We can safely divide them into three classes:

1. Those who naturally were gentle, kind, and tenderhearted, but by reason of their brutalizing and humiliating confinement lost all traces of their finer sensibilities.

2. Those who began their prison life with strange streaks in their make-ups, who are released with their natural weaknesses so accentuated and intensified as to baffle analysis.

3. Those who are naturally ugly, morose, sly, cruel, and treacherous — men who believed nothing, cared for nothing, feared nothing, stopped at nothing, and who are released "state-made wild men."

It will be said that the men I have placed in Class 3 might better be locked up for life — that they are hopeless. Again, facts do not bear out any such theory. Many of the most amazing reformations of criminals have occurred among just such men.

But to get back to Billy's Cellar — back to "close-ups" of these men, back to living examples of our prison products, back to facts, *for it is facts we want.*

★

The speaker is a sullen, ugly-looking chap, who bears unmistakably those marks which long years of prison life stamp on a face — deep pallor and a vacant stare.

"Dere wus a guy in de warden's office — 'Beans,' der yer remember 'Beansy,' Joe? He put me wise as ter how I could git me whiskey for lots less money. Well, say, dat wuz me all over. O' course, I changed me liquor dealer right away.

"De guard in de wagon shop got sore de minute I quit fer he knowed blame well I hadn't swore off, and dat somebody wus cuttin' in on his graft. But he couldn't git wise as ter how or where I wus gittin' de stuff. He tried fer a couple a'weeks, but he didn't t'ink I knowed it. Say, I knowed de foist move he made. At de end a'two weeks he wus boilin' mad, fer another lad quit him an' got his booze like I wus gittin' mine. O' course I got blamed fer de loss a'dat customer, too, but I didn't have nuthin' ter do wid it.

"All dis time de guard didn't say nuttin' ter me, but de way he kept lookin' at me I knowed somet'ing wus comin' ter me.

"One mornin', when de company went down wid de buckets, dey kept me locked in. Dere wus t'ree of 'em. When dey got done yer wouldn't a'knowed de coop. Did dey find any booze? Dey did not! I knowed me little game too well.

"De next mornin' dey kept me locked in again. Only two come dis time. An', say, what dey didn't do ter me wasn't never done ter noboddy. Foist dey put de nippers on me. Den dey give me de woist beatin' I ever got, an' I'se had some good ones. Dey punched me back and forth between 'em! Dey landed on me anywhere! Four or five times dey knocked me down! Dey kicked me in de face an' stomick! Dey didn't care — dey didn't feel it. It lasted fifteen minutes.

"Dey left me, den — but dey hadn't said a woid. Dey didn't have ter, dough, fer a little boid whispered in me right ear — I t'ink it wus a' English sparrow.

"So de next day I changed me liquor dealer again an' de other guy he did de same, fer de little boid what told me, told him, too."

ch. ends p. 130

★

There is, of course, the other side — the sad attempt to bring religion to men forced to live as convicts live, amid graft and silence, and armed guards, and a system entirely repressive. But listen to the way this attempt works out in a very high percentage of cases. It is Billy talking — Billy, of Billy's Cellar:

"Back in de old days — an' I guess it's de same now — a guy could git a Bible fer a wink o' de eye. Der wus hundreds of 'em.

"Yer know, all de time dey wus paddlin' us on bare backs wid leather straps till de blood ran, while dey wus killin' us in de cooler, an' while dey wus stringin' us up by de t'umbs or de wrists, dey wus preachin' on Sunday out a' de Bible. Tellin' us how good God wus — an' how He loved us; tellin' us about de Golden Rule, an' how we ought ter love our brothers, our fellowmen. An' speakin' about love an' de Golden Rule — say, man, yer could a'jumped out a' de Chaplin's office onter de death house an' de electric chair. Dat's how near dat guy lived ter de Golden Rule!

"An' der yer know dat in de Chapel, where de armed 'screws' used ter stand watch over us at gospel service, wus a sign — 'God is good; God is love.' Say, all de love an' goodness we seen up in dat whole blame dump wus in dat sign. Anyhow, dere wus loads a' Bibles.

"Me an' Jack used ter sneak a bit o' ham or bacon or a' egg or two inter de cell at lock-up. We'd take de stuff in under our coats or in our pants. As soon as t'ings got quiet, after dey took de 'count,' Jack 'u'd take his stool an' sit at de cell door ter watch. If anybody come along he'd open a book or a paper ter screen off de back a' de cell.

"When Jack give me de woid I'd git out de grub an' me pan.

"'Who did yer cremate last night, Billy?' Jack always began wid dat. 'Try St. Luke wit' de eggs ter-night — it's a grand combination!'

"An' I'd tear out page after page a' de Bible an' hold 'em, boinin', in me fingers till de stuff wus what we called done. Sure, it wus slow goin'.

"I used ter laugh when I'd be pullin' a Bible ter bits how fooled de people wus what sent dem books up. I could hear de sky pilots readin' reports ter de church people about how many men dere wus in 'stir' and how many of 'em wus usin' Bibles. I wish he'd 'a' told 'em what use most of 'em wus put ter."

★

Tommy S—— has a bad leg and a worse back. He is telling of Sing Sing and more particularly of the Principal Keeper-in-charge at the time he was rendered "no account" for the rest of his life.

"I mean what I say! Anybody can be hard when he wants ter, but nobody could be like *he* wus widout years o' gittin' used ter it. He had his heart wore out years before I even seen him. He's dead now, God have mercy on his soul! Hardship or cruelty or sufferin' — dem t'ings didn't mean no more ter him dan dried apples, chewin' gum, or soap. He could order a poor guy t'rown inter de cooler an' t'ink no more about it dan if you or me told a small boy he couldn't have no more cake. He could say, 'Take him down fer ten days,' widout battin' an eye. He did it so often it didn't mean nuttin' ter him no more.

"But it meant so much ter de boys what served under him dat he never dared walk around de yard or de shop widout he had a couple o' 'screws' along wid him. An' in de thirty-five years he held his job he never dared to come down ter New York City — dere wus too many who would 'a' 'croaked' him.

ch. ends p. 130

"De two worst cases o' de cooler I ever got come ter me — one fer talk in' in de shop an' oncet fer cuttin' a guy. Fer de little t'ings an' de big t'ings yer got de cooler. It wus de easiest way.

"If yer had a' argument wid a lad an' he had a pull or de 'screw' wus after yer, away yer went ter de cooler — half de time not knowin' what fer an' not gettin' a chance ter find out or ter say anyt'ing.

"De last time dey t'rew me in wus fer de cuttin' job. I wus near wild wid anger. I hollered an' cussed fer two whole days an' nights. Den I wus wore out. I couldn't stand no more. I lay on de bare, damp stone floor. Dere wus no bed or chair or anyt'ing. It took five 'screws' ter put me in de dump. But in two days I hadn't de strength of a baby. Dey nearly beat de life out o' me before dey left me.

"Once in twenty-four hours dey shoved in a slice o' bread an' a gill o' water, an' me burnin' up wid fever. But dey didn't know it an' I wus too sick to tell 'em.

"Fer fourteen days and fourteen nights I lay dere. When dey looked in at me dat day dey couldn't see me breathe, so dey called de doctor. He took one look at me an' beat it fer de office an' told de P. K. ter take me out or I'd 'kick out.'

"Let de _____ die!" said the P. K. I learned dis later from a trusty.

"Finally, near night, de doctor ordered me out himself — I wus dat near dead. Dey had ter lift me on a stretcher. Fer four months I wus sick in de hospital. Dat's ten years ago! Look at me now!"

*

As fearful almost as any punishment is the monotonous prison life itself. The enforced silence, the nerve-racking, eternal spying makes life worse than death. The mind stagnates. The soul becomes buried in a mildew of wretch-edness. The animal replaces the man.

There is but one way to escape this dreadful demoralizing monotony. It is by a transfer to the hospital. The eagerness with which men crave a "ticket" (an order to the hospital) is well illustrated by the experience of a man I'll call Ed:

"After one o' me stays in de cooler, dey t'rew me han'cuffed inter a cell on de 'Flats' (the ground floor of the cell block at Sing Sing where there is always moisture and mildew). I wus dere fer thirteen days an' nights wearin' dem bracelets, too. Yer know how well I could take care o' meself wearin' dem t'ings, don't yer?

"I wus about crazy before dey let me out. De sight o' de yard or de shops would 'a' drove me clean nutty. I couldn't bear de t'ought o' goin' back ter it all, much as I wanted ter git out o' de 'Flats.'

"De hospital fer me, says I. But before I made up me mind how ter work it dey sent me back ter me bench in de shoe shop.

"As quick as I got dere an idea come inter me mind. I grabbed me knife from de bench in front o' me an' put it on de oil-stone an' give it a good edge. Den I laid it on de end o' me left t'umb, holdin' it wid me right hand.

"Next ter me wus a big nigger — Nigger Sam. I seen him lookin' at me, an' I says, under me breath, 'Sam, hit de knife a good clip wid yer hammer.'

"An' Sam did! He did it like I had a' asked him ter open a window, or move out a' der way. He didn't even blink his eyes, an' he didn't look at de mess after he done it.

"I wrapped up de good end of me t'umb in a big red handkerchief an' stuck it up in de air ter let 'em know I wanted ter speak to 'em.

"It did de trick, all right, an' fer a week I lived in de hos-pital, an' fer another week I had ter go over every day ter git me t'umb dressed."

ch. ends next p.

*

The prison of tomorrow must be a better one than the prison of today.

> Horace W. Scandlin
> *World Outlook*
> February 1920

Aaron W Scandlin

What of John Goode?

FEW autobiographies published in recent years and dealing with the miracle of grace which transforms the heart and life of the sinner have attracted more attention or elicited more cordial approval than "The Wicked John Goode." The publication in a recent issue of the Christian Herald of a letter from a New Hampshire reader, calling in question the wisdom and spiritual profit of publishing the characters of bad men in connection with the operation of the Holy Spirit in their redemption, has stirred up a number of other readers to send us their views on the subject. We are glad to publish these letters, and will be equally pleased to give space to the opposite view in such a controversy. John Goode's story is one that needs no defense at our hands; it is one of the greatest and most convincing object-lessons, showing that we have a Saviour who "saves to the uttermost." We give some of these letters below:

"I have read the comment on John Goode by a reader in New Hampshire, questioning the wisdom and spiritual profit to be derived from such characters. Well, I differ and hold the contrary. His story warns others from traveling the same path. It shows that 'the way of the transgressor is hard,' and it glorifies God, who is able to save to the uttermost. I thank you very much for the story.
"*Peterson, Minn.* J. C. D."

"I have just finished reading the story of 'The Wicked John Goode.' What a mighty struggle with the demon drink, rising and falling, again and again, at last gaining the victory, by the grace of God, through the instrumentality of Dr. Hallimond and the other noble men who took him by the hand, calling him 'brother,' patiently bearing with his backslidings and not casting him off as a hopeless case! Surely there will be stars in their crowns for their noble work! And now John Goode, redeemed and cleansed, is trying to lead others to the Cross and to accept his Saviour as their Saviour. May God bless the Bowery Mission, where many a degraded one has been happily saved and restored to loved ones! Dr. Hallimond and his helpers have many discouragements, but courage and patience and a friendly hand and an earnest prayer bring their reward.
"*Troy, N. Y.* SUBSCRIBER."

"I looked forward from week to week to the story of John Goode. Now that it is finished, I, with others, want to change his name to 'John Did Me Good.' It is a wonderful account of sin at its worst and salvation at its best. It is not every one upon whose mind experiences make such a vivid impression that they can afterward be described so tellingly.
"*Wyncote, Pa.* LAURENCE S."

"The serial, 'John Goode,' is the best thing in a long time. It is a great demonstration of what divine grace can do, and it should be a great help and encouragement to the faithful workers of the Bowery Mission and its supporters.
"*Richland, N. Y.* L. F."

"I have just read the last chapter of 'The Wicked John Goode.' I do not care for continued stories, even in religious papers, but this has been an exception. I only wish there was more of it. It has made my heart overflow with joy to know that God is so good while men are so wicked, and that he is long-suffering while men continue in sin. This has been one of the most interesting things I have ever read. I love to read about men being saved from sin. I think it would be a good thing if this story could be brought out in book form. I am sending this [$5], and hope and pray that it may be used to God's glory in saving some men who are down and out and making them useful men, clean, sober and honest—men who, after they have been saved, will be the means of the salvation of others. Second, that it may help to give those hungry men some food. I do not know what it means to be hungry; but I do hope I hunger to be a better man. Also if it may help warm some poor, cold fellow, the sending of this will be a joy to me. May the Lord use it to make some heart as glad as mine. May he greatly bless the Bowery Mission and its noble workers. Pray for me.
"*Haines, Ore.* C. W. H."

"The story of John Goode should be put in book form and sent broadcast over New York and every other city in the United States. It is such lives in their saddest, blackest, most pitiful phase, which are underlying all the other strata of society—one that the business world should stamp out in its own interests. The suggestion made by John Goode—that there be places provided where a man, down and out, could get a clean 'pad' to sleep on and sanitary conditions in which to wash for 10 cents a night (and that could be made to pay expenses) should be looked into and acted on. To walk the streets in thin clothing all night rather than sleep (or only lie down under cover), and to get up nauseated with foul air and alive with vile vermin, is enough to force a man to spend his next 5 cents in a drink. The very repulsion of even such wretches shows there is a spark of decency left.
"Cannot the Christian Herald air the idea? Will not some one take the place of Jacob Riis, and start the movement? I will head the list with $10, and help till it is on a paying basis—though I am old and poor.
"*Newark, N. J.* FRIEND."

It will gladden many hearts to know that John Goode is telling to audiences in churches of different denominations the story of his wonderful transformation and is everywhere received with cordial appreciation. Pastors are writing to us, arranging for their congregations to hear the story of this new messenger of grace. It is one which cannot fail to inspire any Christian audience with the desire to follow the example of the Master, and to go out into the "highways and byways" to find the lost. This is an essential part of the true mission of the Church of Christ, and John Goode is proving a most efficient helper.

www.ingramcontent.com/pod-product-compliance
Lightning Source LLC
Chambersburg PA
CBHW022058020426

42335CB00012B/735